PEARLS OF WISDOM

For Living a Richer Life

Compiled by
Patricia Crane, Ph.D.
and
Rick Nichols

The
Crane's Nest

The information in this book is designed to impart information to help individuals in making positive changes in their lives. The ideas presented are not meant to substitute for medical care or psychological assistance.

Published by:
The Crane's Nest, a division of Health Horizons.
P.O. Box 1081
Bonsall, California, 92003
(800) 969–4584
www.heartinspired.com

ISBN: 1-893705-19-6 - $14.95
Self Help/Inspirational

DEDICATION

This book is dedicated to all of the authors whose stories are contained within these pages. They shared honestly and openly from their experiences so that others might benefit from their wisdom. May their words inspire you and assist you on your path.

Contents

Acknowledgments

Over the last several years, we were often asked, "how did you do it?" when people discovered that Rick and I had each published a book. Most of the people we spoke to also wanted to publish a book, but had little idea of the process. So they began suggesting that we publish an anthology of stories. We thank those who kept reminding us that we said it was a wonderful idea. One day Patricia finally put together the email to send out about the project. Through the amazing technology we call the internet, thousands of people around the globe were offered the opportunity to be included in this book. We had no idea what would happen, but within hours we had more than enough responses to fill not just one, but two books! We thank all the authors who took the time to write their stories and meet our deadlines as well as they did.

We appreciate the efforts of our editor Bobbie Probstein, also an author and dear friend. In the midst of a busy holiday season she managed to focus on each story and help craft it into a stronger contribution. We also thank our personal assistant, Stephanie Swink, who read the final drafts of each story and still found those little typos and grammatical errors we had all missed. Her usual career these days is professional organizing (and she is very good at it) so we appreciate the time she diverted to help us with the last phase of the book. Since publishing Patricia's book only four years ago, the industry standard for submitting a book to a printer has changed to InDesign, a program Rick hadn't used previously. He is grateful to Kera McHugh, also our webmaster, who patiently walked him through some of the elements of this new program. We are also grateful to Steve Pawlacyk of Media Lithographics, Inc. for his invaluable assistance in liberating these words from our computers and setting them free to do their work in the world through this book. Finally, we thank our families and friends for their ongoing support. While not directly involved in this project, their love and positive energy assist us in all that we do.

INTRODUCTION

While traveling and teaching personal growth workshops worldwide, we have noted that people in every country, at the core of their being, want the same things: meaning in life, happiness, and peace. The powerful stories in this book, contributed from ten countries and twelve states in the US, support that observation. You will read of challenges with health, relationships, finances, career, and self-esteem. More importantly you will read of the triumphs in overcoming those adversities. The authors share honestly and intimately about the obstacles they overcame on the passage towards the life of their dreams. They recount their healing journeys emotionally, spiritually, and physically. Their stories will inspire you with their courage and determination. Through these pages it is our desire that you find exactly what you need at this time in your life to inspire you with the possibility of creating the life you want.

For the most part, the authors in this book are not professional writers, but all of them are engaged in fulfilling work that is designed to help others heal on every level. About half of them have trained with us as Heal Your Life, Achieve Your Dreams workshop leaders. They are everyday people from a multiplicity of cultures, education, ethnicities, and nationalities. They represent a rich mix of backgrounds and points of view. Therefore, in reviewing the materials submitted for this anthology we were immediately reminded of the reality that the English language is not the same to all people. The British, Australians, Canadians, Irish, Scotts, New Yorkers, and Californians all speak and write slightly different versions of it. Not to mention the authors for whom English is not their native language. This can be a challenge when compiling a book with such language and cultural diversities. In all fairness, whose English language do we use?

The biggest challenge we have all around the world is non-acceptance of the differences in peoples, their belief systems, and their ways of doing things. We feel the world would be a much more peaceful place to live in if we could honor the differences in people and cultures rather than trying to change everything to match our own way of being and doing. In order to support the idea of unity, acceptance and tolerance of diverse ways, we decided to be as open as possible to these differences during the editorial process. We have also been careful to allow the personalities of the authors to shine through their words. To prepare you for the differences in spelling, punctuation, colloquialisms, and sentence structure you will find the authors' name along with their home country or state directly beneath the title of each story.

It has been a pleasure for us to compile this anthology. We suspect that you may find just the right insight on the following pages to move you in one way or another toward a happier, more fulfilled life. If not that, then at least we know that you will enjoy these lovely pearls of wisdom from our everyday sages.

Love and blessings,

Patricia & Rick

January 23, 2006
San Diego, California

G IS FOR GRATITUDE

Michele Hatfield Quesenberry, Maryland

*"I created a fun way to condition my
mind to see the good in life. . ."*

Life is all about perspective; it's your choice how to see it. Over the last 15 years my perspective of the world has changed dramatically. Back then, I lived in misery, believing the outside world determined my life experiences. A common phrase used to describe how I felt: *hating life.* Now it is: *passion for life!* I proudly display my current mode of operation with a personalized license plate: LOV2LIV. Being the co-creator of my life, I'm tickled to catch other drivers smiling in my direction as I grin with joy behind the wheel. This transformation wasn't quick or easy; however, I created a fun way to condition my mind to see the good in life. I invented a game called *The Gralphabet™.*

The Gralphabet™ *(gral`fa bet`), n. a system of characters or signs in alphabetical order with which the language of gratitude is expressed.* Ex. A - I am grateful for *apples* because they are scrumptiously tasty and a healthy

1

snack. B-I am grateful for *breathing* because it gives me life. C - I'm grateful for *cartoons* because they give me a good *chuckle...* I got a double! I'm grateful for chuckling too. D - ...

The Universe responds to thoughts and beliefs. What I decide to focus on is exactly what I'm going to see. When hating life was my motto, I saw people were out to get me, out to better themselves by using me. I believed I didn't need people for anything and pushed them far, far away. I thought I was tough and didn't care how much pain I had to endure to prove to the world that I could handle it on my own. Of course the result was a feeling of emptiness, a gaping hole of loneliness that I pretended wasn't there, yet felt so deeply. I blamed life for doing this to me instead of acknowledging that my feelings were only a reflection of the thoughts and beliefs I projected outward. Negativity consumed my mind and I allowed it to have power over me.

One day, the avoidance of misery stopped. I caught myself in the mirror and saw an empty shell of human flesh, a young woman who hated herself and felt unworthy of love or friendship. Something deep inside knew that wasn't true, yet tears began to flow. I had been so tough for so long that once I opened the door to feel the pain, the floodgates opened; I sobbed for days. I knew I didn't want the rest of my life to feel that empty or else I wanted my life to end. I had found the cold, dark empty space that was longing to love and be loved.

A few months later, beginning to awaken my consciousness with a handful of self-help books, I finally reached out for help. A friend introduced me to someone who was willing to support my growth as long as I was willing to listen to her advice. She saw my pain more clearly than I did and gave me an assignment: "Write down twenty things a day that you are grateful for."

TWENTY things, I thought. *How can I think of twenty things when I can barely think of two or three?* The challenge took a couple of weeks to overcome procrastination. Finally, desperate to get out of myself, I began.

Every night I searched my mind to come up with something to be grateful for. In a few weeks my closed little mind began opening. The more I sought gratitude, the more I realized how much abundance there was in life and how I'd taken so much for granted. My mother took me in after six years of being on my own when I hadn't cared to share much of my life with her. There was a roof over my head, a comfortable bed to sleep in and blankets to keep me warm. At times, when I didn't have money for lunch, co-workers would share so I wouldn't go hungry. My boss allowed me to make my own schedule and study on the clock during down time. The community even supported me with public transportation, as my car often broke down. Not only did I need people, I started to see how much I relied on them.

Practicing gratitude enlightened me in so many ways. For the first time I pondered how miraculous life really was: amazing how much energy and effort went into the smallest things! Giving thanks at mealtime turned into a feast of appreciation for the sun, the rain, the seeds, the trees, the wind, the soil . . . all of Mother Nature. The number of hands and physical bodies it took to have food in front of me were countless. The farmers, the inventors of tractors and machinery, assembly line workers, drivers, chefs, marketers and even the grocery store clerk. The list would go on and on! Expressing gratitude brought so much fun and joy that I created a game to experience that overflowing affection, awe and appreciation any time of the day.

3

The Gralphabet helped me see the positive, and helped me feel and experience the abundance of love and support in the world, even during a tough run or long drive. It kept me centered and trained my mind to automatically seek *what* and *why* to be grateful—changing focus from what I didn't like to what I really loved. Many things I had seen as ugly or negative now had beautiful or positive attributes. All I had to do was ask one question: What can I be grateful for?

That gaping hole inside me was now full. Life transformed because I changed my view and the Universe was responding. I played the game on my own and often shared with others. I made it even more fun by challenging myself to think of two or three things per letter. Thoughts popped all day long with a resounding: *Yes! I'm grateful for that too!*

Over the years I learned to say the entire Gralphabet for a specific topic, like my body, a holiday or Mother Earth and discovered an abundance of things I'd previously taken for granted. Writing the Gralphabet for someone special has proven to delight another's heart for a lifetime. Children love the game and are guaranteed to remind you over and over again how to play.

Every time I ponder the miracles that happen in my own little body, I'm overwhelmed with joy and appreciation for life. Shifting that same contemplation to family and friends, to God, to Mother Nature, the planet, the Universe, I realize miracles are just endless. The attitude of gratitude has transformed my life. The more abundance and miracles I see the more abundantly and miraculously the Universe responds. I am eternally grateful and absolutely LOV2LIV!

Let's do the Gralphabet!

I'm grateful for:

A - The incredible **Abundance** life offers just for the asking!

B - The **Beautiful Blossoms** the earth so graciously gives us!

C - The endless flow of **Creativity**!

D - **Dancing** vivaciously!

E - **Energy** in motion… **E-motion**!

F - **Forgiveness**, a constant letting go!

G - **Gratitude!** There can never be enough thanks!

H - **Holding Hands**, such a gentle loving gesture!

I - **Intimacy**! In-to-me (or you)… see?

J - **Jumping** with **Joy**!

K - Random acts of **Kindness**!

L - **Love**! The ultimate healer!

M - **Mistakes!** The greatest teacher!

N - **Nature!** What an amazing kingdom!

O - **Oxygen** because we are deep breathing and alive!

P - **Prayer**, incredible communication with Spirit!

Q - **Quarrels!** No differences would be boring!

R - **Rest** and **Relaxation**! Time to **Rejuvenate**!

S - **Silliness**! Lighten up with a **Silly Smile**!

T - **Tears**, a natural way to release sadness or sorrow and express great joys!

U - **Universal** Wisdom! A higher connection words cannot describe!

V - Vision! What a powerful tool our Creator gave us!

W - Wonder! Being in awe of the world!

X - X-chromosome! Life is more fun with two sexes!

Y - You! You are unique and you make a difference!

Z - Zeal, an extraordinary enthusiasm for life!

Try it out for yourself—Go through the letters of the alphabet, state what you're grateful for and why. Have fun conditioning your mind to be even more grateful!

THE CANYON
Rev. Christine Green, Oregon

"I realized I wasn't alone in this life transition, and had an experience of being part of a divine plan. . ."

After nine years, it was over. After much soul searching, counseling, coaching, and processing, I ended the nine-year relationship. There wasn't any one significant thing that brought it to an end, but many small things that never seemed to be resolved. We had grown apart, had different goals and were on different paths.

So here I was on my own, just two weeks before my 35th birthday. I found a place to live with two roommates in a large, roomy house. Not only did I move to a new place, but was also looking for a new job. Everything was changing. I felt like Dorothy in the Wizard of Oz. "Toto, something tells me we're not in Kansas anymore." All that was familiar was gone; I was putting one foot in front of the other trying to figure out my next steps.

I stood in the middle of my new bedroom surrounded by boxes. Feeling the freedom of being out of the struggle and strife I thought to myself: *How great, I'm on my own!,* and gasped at the realization that the freedom was also the absence of all that was familiar. I could feel my fear of the unknown in the pit of my stomach and thought in the same breath, *Oh no, I'm on my own! How will I ever find the courage to move forward?* For the next two weeks I woke up around 2:00 a.m. and stayed awake the rest of the night. The house I lived in was drafty and noisy and the two roommates were on very different paths. I felt such turmoil and so alone.

The only comfort I found in that environment was in the backyard; at the edge was a canyon. To anyone else, it was just a canyon. To me, it was glorious . . . my own private sanctuary. Early each Saturday morning, I would take a little folding beach chair across the lawn to the edge, wrap a blanket around me to keep off the early morning chill and . . . breathe. It was so easy to breathe in the softness, for nature has its own perfume, subtle and powerful. I watched the eucalyptus trees bending and swaying in the breeze. The birds performed their own ballet, moving gracefully from tree to tree. I suppose there was nothing unusual or unique about how the canyon looked, but the beauty I experienced was a feeling. Thomas Moore writes in *Care for the Soul,* "An appreciation for beauty is simply openness to the power of things to stir the soul. If we can be affected by beauty, then soul is alive and well in us, because the soul's great talent is for being affected."

In that precious time at the canyon, I was able to set aside all my cares and concerns. It provided insights that supported my healing process. The first insight was **Gratitude**. Instead of looking at the things that weren't working, I began to feel gratitude for the gifts and blessings I had. Gratitude is like the telephoto lens on a camera, bringing a subject closer with clarity. By focusing my attention on the wonders of nature, I felt deep gratitude and appreciation for all the things that were working in my life.

I had an extraordinary feeling of **Oneness**, no longer feeling alone but now part of the universal wholeness. My breath became one with the air. I realized I wasn't alone in this life transition, and had an experience of being part of a divine plan. "I know the plans I have for you," declares the Lord, "plans to prosper you and not harm you. Plans to give you hope and a future."

After years of trying to hold things together in my relationship, I knew I had to let go of control. The relationship was finished—nothing more to fix, manage or manipulate. It was time to **Surrender** what my human personality wanted and move into a new experience of **Faith** and trust in Spirit to guide me in the days ahead.

How can one observe the extraordinary beauty, amazing order and the powerful experience that nature brings forth and not feel **Love**? Love is the experience where nothing is missing or broken and everything is possible. The beauty of nature stirs the healing presence of love to come forth. From Joel Goldsmith, in *Practicing the Presence,* "Love this world; love the sun, the moon, the stars; love the plants and the flowers; love all the people. Let the love flow. That love which flows out from the infinite storehouse within you will be the bread of life which will come back to you."

The canyon became everything I needed: a meditation room, classroom, a place of devotion and healing . . . my sanctuary. It helped me recognize and realize gratitude, oneness, surrender, faith and love. I only lived there eight months yet those lessons never left. It was glorious!

TODAY IS THE DAY I MEET MY SOUL MATE

Renée Montemayor, England

*"I decided if he wasn't going to love me
I had to learn to love myself. . ."*

By 1996 I had been in a serious relationship with my boyfriend for nearly two years. We loved each other, making plans to live together and had even discussed marriage. I had no idea that just after my 21st birthday, I'd be catapulted into my own personal hell—no indication a petty argument one morning would be the catalyst to change the trajectory of my life forever.

There was nothing unusual about that morning as I prepared breakfast. We'd started to row about something so insignificant that now, in retrospect, I can't even remember what it was about. It escalated into a full-blown argument right before I'd had to rush off to go to an audition, which, consequently, I failed.

Upset, I called him, expecting to be comforted and half-expecting we'd resolve our differences from that morning's misunderstandings. However, he had a different agenda . . . I discovered he wanted to break up!

I tried to remain calm and felt he was being totally irrational and melodramatic. However, he'd absolutely made up his mind and proceeded to dump me. As the days progressed I realised he was deadly serious and going to make this split the most unbearable, messy and humiliating experience for me that he could. He was on a rampage to vent his anger. Love turned to hate and it showed in his eyes. Where was this coming from? It was a frightening case of *'Jekyll and Hyde'*. This was war, and I felt mortally wounded.

When it became undeniably apparent he was never coming back I had to deal with a triple measure of pain: the separation, being unemployed and finally having to confront my eating disorder, which I'd kept secret for years. All this compounded my already low self-esteem. I hit rock bottom and felt worthless.

I felt so depressed it was difficult to execute even the most basic day-to-day tasks. Each minute felt excruciating without him. I couldn't eat or sleep and developed an uncontrollable twitch in my leg. I had all the classic symptoms of a nervous breakdown and wanted to commit suicide. My parents were so worried they considered finding me professional help.

Instead, I chose to fight for my life because mother had challenged my courage. I decided if he wasn't going to love me I had to learn to love myself.

I'd always been a searcher since childhood and acquired a varied collection of psychological, metaphysical and spiritual books. If there ever was a time I needed to refer to them it was now. I needed to understand and actually apply these philosophies and devoured every book, but this time I actually followed the exercises and meditations suggested because my life literally depended on it. I felt comforted and soothed by the thought that whoever had written these books understood my pain. I wrote honestly in my journals and often lulled myself to sleep clutching tear-stained pages, and in my darkest nights, when I felt most alone, I would close my eyes and pray to God and my guardian angels, mentally screaming the words *HELP ME!*

Over the course of 9 months I became proactive in helping my soul heal and seeking spirituality. I desperately needed to understand myself. I felt guided to go to spiritualist churches and meet a variety of different healers, psychics, channellers, and mediums and reached out to gain support from family and friends. I took responsibility of my own healing process by praying and meditating daily. I became disciplined at meditating every morning, noon and night.

The option to kill myself rapidly disappeared as I learned if I did my soul would still remain in pain, albeit in another dimension. Despite fear I encouraged my heart to stay open and asked, *what do you long for?* It replied: *I want you to love and accept me just as I am.*

In that security I believed I'd attract a man who would truly love me unconditionally. *No more self-punishment,* I promised. I forced myself to eat properly and took the first tenuous steps to learn to love myself. I didn't appreciate it at the time, but my ex-boyfriend had given me the opportunity to transform my life. Death or Rebirth? My choice.

I was told: *if you love something let it go and if it returns to you it's yours to keep, but if it doesn't it was never yours to begin with.* I found this statement haunting me time and time again, through books I'd read, people I'd meet, and even once found it etched into the door of a toilet cubicle, staring back at me! I began to notice that synchronisms like these were occurring more often; encouraging me to continue what I was doing.

Life became an adventure. I became the most important person in my life, not him, and began to like myself. As energy and confidence grew, I began to love myself, linking with my future self often and asking the future Renée, who got it right: *Sister…how did you do it? Show me the way. Guide me to live the life of my dreams with my perfect match. Show me how to find him…."*

Surrendering my will to the Divine will was tough. I often repeated: *Your will, not mine Lord…I trust, I trust, I trust . . .* while looking up hopefully at the sky and courageously letting go of the outcome. It strengthened my faith. I stayed open to all possibilities, yet a tiny part remained in the hope my ex would realise his mistake and come running back. The Universe had other plans.

"Today is the day I meet my soul mate." I repeated this affirmation over and over in excited anticipation: the one perfect statement crafted for me. It got me emotionally excited and instantly optimistic, believing with each repetition my ideal partner was magnetically being drawn closer. Wherever and whatever I was doing I'd mentally be chanting it in my head. *Today is the day I meet my soul mate…today is the day I meet my soul mate…today is the day I meet my soul mate…* I became so good at believing it, I'd wake up every morning eager at the prospect that indeed this might well be the day I'd meet him…so I'd better be ready! I started to make an effort to look nice, just in case. Like a movie in my mind I would imagine he'd be the next one to board whatever bus or train I was on, or be the person to walk through the door of wherever I was. I paid attention to all my interactions with other people. *Who is this mystery guy?* I wondered. I managed to turn my situation around, feeling empowered. Life became exciting as I viewed each day as a possible magical encounter. I became radiant and people began reacting to me differently. I loved it.

Then one day I got a call from the producers of a hit London West End show with an offer of work. Would I be willing to come back for a while and help them out as one of the cast members had gotten pregnant? Would I? Yes! Of course I would!

In February 1997, the new cast rehearsed. The director paired us into dance partners and put me together with a very handsome and talented actor called Julian, then changed his mind and moved us around. As I was led away from Julian I felt my energy instantly drop and thought, *that's strange*. Unknown to me, Julian had also felt the same thing at that precise moment. There was definitely chemistry between us.

We got to know each other as much as we could before my contract expired. We enjoyed each other's company and found ourselves remaining in cafes and restaurants until they closed, laughing, talking and philosophising about life until the early hours of the morning, and discovered we had very similar beliefs. We were unashamedly candid with each other discussing ex-partners and very personal fears, hopes and dreams. We realised that 'coincidentally' Julian had unknowingly been living in my area for a few months. He had moved there after his separation from his long-term girlfriend who had kicked him out of her flat! It was as if the Universe had been playing a game with us, intentionally manoeuvring us closer together on the chequerboard of life.

A whole array of synchronisms started to manifest whenever we were together. One after the other, something else would confirm he was indeed the gift the universe had been preparing and now wanted me to accept. Time seemed to accelerate. We felt like we were caught up in a beautiful and magical whirlwind. Neither of us wanted it to stop so we went along with it trusting the process, and each other, every step of the way. *What a good and beautiful man*, I thought, *he has such a beautiful heart and soul (and what a bonus, he's also really sexy!)* What more could I ask for? I had it all. He was everything on my 'list' and more! The attraction was so powerful that only two weeks later we admitted our love for each other, and moved in together. And four months later we married!

We've been together now for 9 extraordinary years, experiencing good times and bad times, yet remaining strong. I'm proud of us; we're both only 30 years old and we're enjoying the most passionate, exciting, beautiful, and fulfilling marriage that anyone could ever wish for. We have a deep and spiritual connection with love, respect and trust. He's my best-friend, husband, lover, earth angel, and partner in every sense.

I am indeed married to my soul mate and our relationship continues to grow and deepen over the years. We feel blessed to have found each other, for we know we have what most people are searching for. And every night as I lay my head on my pillow I acknowledge all this to the Divine and with gratitude in my heart whisper, "Thank you."

SEVEN MAGICAL WORDS

Barbara Avril Burgess, England

*"I even found myself falling asleep with a smile
on my face and waking up the same. . ."*

I've known about affirmations for a number of years and given them a try. Like many people, I am a very impatient person, and if something doesn't work straight away, I either forget about it or stop doing it.

I tried doing them, read books about them, looked them up on web sites and attended workshops where they were used. I suppose at the time I could have said they didn't work for me, but that would be incorrect. They did in fact work but it took a long time, or rather I took a long time, for the message to 'sink in.' I didn't realise at the time that they were in fact changing my life slowly but surely; I just hadn't noticed any big difference. It was a subtle change but definitely a change for the better!

As I said, I'm impatient. I had a go at using many different affirmations. One of the most famous or well known is 'I am getting better and better and better.' I

16

said this affirmation when I felt like it and when I remembered. I did not say it all the time and thought it wasn't working, but with hindsight, even though I didn't say it all the time, it did work; and I *have* gotten better and better and better.

I guess I first learned about affirmations almost 10 years ago. I read the books and listened to the tapes and then forgot about them. I am the kind of person who will watch an exercise video whilst doing the ironing! So the affirmations were stored in my subconscious and the tapes and the books were put on the shelves. However, as I said, I brought them out of the closet on several occasions and they began to work . . . slowly. They may well have worked much quicker if I had continuously used them.

I did get fitter; I did become happier and did find myself healthier, although wealth just eluded me. Actually, the more I seemed to concentrate on wealth the less I had. It was like one step forward and three back; I would say an affirmation and perhaps have a cheque come through the door but then an even bigger bill would come with the next postal delivery! I just didn't know what I was doing wrong. I actually got really fed up with the affirmations and thought they'd never work.

Then, about 6 months ago 'I got it'. In his books, Dr. Phil McGraw talks about people 'getting it' and Patricia Crane and Louise Hay also talk about patience, something I often lack. What made me 'get it' was a friend who gave me some words he said were the *language* of the subconscious or unconscious mind. I've now discovered or realised that what we say is so important. Louise Hay also points this out in her tapes and books. I was going around saying; 'I can't sleep. I've got no money. I'm bored. I'm fed up. I hate wet days,' and do you know what? I produced more of it! What I finally 'got' was that 'we create our own lives'.

I put these two newly rediscovered wisdoms together: we create our own lives with the words we feed to the subconscious mind. I wrote new affirmations and started again! I've become quite good at picking myself up, brushing myself off and starting all over again! The words I use to begin my affirmations are 7 really magical words that the subconscious mind understands:

'Now and every moment I am becoming. . . '

Seven is a magical number too! I began making up my own phrases beginning with these 7 words and the change in my life was truly miraculous! The first time I was given them I put them to use and said: *Now and every moment I am becoming better at sleeping.* I slept well on that first night and have slept well ever since. This is really what made me 'get it'. Results were instantaneous! I became *excited* about my 7 magical words, and discovered excitement increases the power of these things too!

I realised I had been creating the world I lived in: the unhappiness and lack of wealth in my own life and the miserable people around me. And so I used the affirmations on this. *NOW and every moment I am creating a wonderful life for myself.* I added other adjectives and made it a game to think of all the adjectives I could add. *NOW and every moment I am creating a fabulous, wonderful, exciting, vibrant life for myself.*

I think you get the picture. Turning the whole thing into a kind of game and bringing the excitement into the equation also adds power to the words. I really was 'getting it'! All the books I'd read on affirmations said to sing and dance your affirmations. I had tried it before and because I only half-heartedly had a go, it hadn't worked that well. Now I really was singing, dancing and laughing my way through my affirmations. I repeated them whilst I walked my dog and said them every night and every morning. I even found myself falling asleep with a smile on my face and waking up the same. For once I was enjoying life!

I was, however, still surrounded by people who were beginning to annoy me. Then I realised that I had created them in my life! I had created all the misery in my life! I also thought: *what is the point if it is only **I** who has the wonderful life, if it's only **me** who is happy?* So off I went with more affirmations: *NOW and every moment I am creating a wonderful life for myself, my family, my friends, my relatives, and my animals.* Then another idea came—why not add the rest of the planet and all that's in it? Why should I be the only one with a wonderful life and why can't this planet of ours be like paradise? I went affirmation mad!

Others that I use are: *NOW and every moment I am becoming richer, fitter, happier, healthier, and wealthier.* And, *NOW and every moment expected and unexpected income is always coming my way.*

The wealth one has worked very quickly too, as have the others. I often go into a shop nowadays and find 3 for 2 or buy one, get one free. I've won three small amounts on the lottery too. A strange thing about two of the lottery wins was, the first was £7 and the second was £21, which is 3 x 7 and 7 is a magical number! It seems that whatever I want to buy is being sold cheaper, whether it's a dress or potatoes! I have also had unexpected cheques come through the post and vouchers too, and the bonus is because I find this so amazing I'm becoming happier and happier.

These 7 words have changed my life completely and are changing the lives of others when they use them. I feel sure they will change and bring magic into your life too!

THE FLOWERING OF HOPE

Laurina Bergqvist, Sweden

"I spent a whole summer checking on
the 'miracle pansy' every day. . ."

It all started with my youngest son's serious illness about two years ago. My life turned into a nightmare of seizures and fear. Even with medication, the nightmare continued, but in a slightly different form. Each day was a struggle. How could I help him and myself? Focused solely on day-to-day survival, I had lost touch with all joy in my life.

In the middle of this emotional and physical distress, I sought solace in my beautiful garden. It became my place of retreat, a place to relax or listen to my inner wisdom. I would walk in my garden all times of the day. Wandering amidst the trees, I turned to them occasionally for friendly advice, or quietly sat next to the creek and just watched the water as it washed past the rocks. I kept my eyes open for signs of wild animals that entered this lovely place. Nevertheless, lately I'd received hope from a more inconspicuous source: a tiny yellow pansy.

Every spring I enjoyed buying a whole flat of pansies to spread color and cheer. I divided and planted them in pots placed throughout my garden. Some years I chose mixed colors; in other years I only selected purple pansies. Usually at the end of their growing season, I would dig small holes in an empty spot in one of my flowerbeds and replant the withering plants there. Each plant would get a second chance, as I hoped to give them another week or two to live. Inevitably their delicate lives ended as winter and frost proved stronger than the pansies. Everyone knew that was the fate of an annual.

Of course, I knew that as well until one bright yellow pansy came back and proved the impossible was possible . . . and it was the same week my youngest son was diagnosed with epilepsy. It had been a terrible winter full of fear. How many times had I held his body as he convulsed? The tears would roll down my cheeks as I prayed for his life and his health.

While walking in my garden right after my son was diagnosed, I spied the little speck of amber—a little yellow pansy had poked its head up through the carpet of brown leaves. Surely, I had planted it there last August, but I'd known it wouldn't survive the harsh winter. Its life span was limited. It was only an annual. As I stood contemplating that flower, I felt such strength and hope emanate from it. *If I can survive the harshest of winters, so can you*, I thought. I could feel the message from the pansy.

I spent a whole summer checking on the "miracle pansy" every day. It gave me hope by demonstrating its own inner strength by surviving, and with its encouragement, I made it through a tough summer.

Although my worries about my son's illness were still with me at summer's end, I lovingly bade farewell to the pansy in August. I was grateful the small flower had returned to share hope and support with me once, but realized it was a one-time miracle.

The second winter was still difficult for my son, but I started finding more inner strength. Yes, I felt slightly stronger now. Perhaps I could handle this situation, this illness. *Maybe,* I told myself.

When spring returned again, I walked in my garden to welcome the lessons that nature would bestow on me. Astounded, I couldn't believe my eyes! The little yellow pansy had survived yet another harsh winter, and returned with its renewed message of hope and strength. Kneeling in the damp earth, I bent over to thank it. Not once, but twice it had overcome insurmountable circumstances. "You, my friend, have inner strength. Thanks for not giving up," I whispered to the pansy.

In the highs and lows to follow, that pansy kept me company every single day. All I had to do was glance at it to feel the smile covering my face and hope rise in my chest. It served as a daily reminder to believe that all things are possible.

Now that another winter has begun, I wonder if the pansy can come back next spring. Fortunately, I now realize, thanks to that miraculous flower, that I can renew my own spirit every spring. No winter is too harsh to break me or erase my joy . . . the joy of a little yellow pansy that keeps coming back and will always grow in my heart.

STILL DADDY'S GIRL!

Rev. La Tonia Muhammad, Washington, DC

"Surrendering my judgments initiated
my forgiveness process, which created
a bridge to the love again. . ."

In October 2005, I lost the first man I ever loved to a massive heart attack . . . my Daddy. My first emotion was shock, then disbelief and absolute horror. I'd talked to him that Sunday morning, but by early evening he was gone from this physical experience. To my dismay, it meant he wouldn't get to see me have my first child, write my first book and launch my coaching career/ministry.

Yes, I'm a daddy's girl. From my earliest memory I loved everything about my father: the way he laughed, his curly hair, tall height and slim fingers, his cooking, intellect and strength of character. My mother tells me he took me everywhere with him and I'd ride by his side. He was proud of me, too—his nickname for me was: "Lady Bird."

The love wasn't always so childlike, however. My relationship with my father represents a journey from childlike adoration to disappointment, pain, fear, forgiveness and then unconditional love. You see, when I was in second grade my father left when he and mother divorced.

When he left her, he left me. I was a child and couldn't separate the act. My world came undone because he took pieces of me with him, and this was the beginning of my feelings of rejection, abandonment and low self-worth. Mother is a strong woman who tried to fill in the gaps of my attachment to him, but she had to process her own pain and betrayal. During this time, therapy wasn't a natural response to life's events. Therefore, as a family we coped and survived. As a child when there's no one to inform you, you do what children do— you make things up! I made up in my mind and heart that since my Daddy didn't stay, he didn't love me.

Had my father forgotten that I was a Daddy's Girl? What happened to the man who took joy and added value by calling his child, Lady Bird? Where was my favorite pal? In my mind this obviously was a case of the body snatchers and I wanted my Daddy back! For years, I tip toed around his trigger-sensitive personality to protect myself. I couldn't help it—I still loved him, and Mother couldn't stand to see my pain.

I hated to "ask" him for anything, including financial support when we really needed it. One harsh tone from my father would resonate through my being and make me nervous and teary, so I developed the habit of NOT ASKING, particularly when the answer was often "No" anyway. The older I got, the less my father gave while my needs grew larger. Somehow, I was still Daddy's Girl, even when it didn't work in my favor.

For the most part, he was absent. I didn't receive counsel from him about dating and courtship, and missed hearing compliments and encouragement from a father, like "You look pretty." or "I like your hair like that." or "You can do it, don't give up." I didn't experi-

REV. LA TONIA MUHAMMAD

ence being held or tears wiped away when I cried, so my deduction was that something was wrong with me and I was certainly NOT pretty and loveable.

Once, when a relative inappropriately touched me, I was angry because I thought my father should be outraged, and he wasn't. I wanted him to make everything all right in my world. Sure, I had my mother who did better than the best she could, and an older sister who served as an angel, but didn't have that father-figure active and engaged in my growth and maturity. Despite all this, I was still my Daddy's girl at the core.

Shortly after my first semester in college, my spirituality began to expand beyond my inherited religion. I asked more questions and journeyed into my personal investigation of The Truth. While undergoing this level of submission to enlightenment, I heard a message that stirred the healing process I'd been asking for in my conversations with God. This "spiritual leader" talked about absent fathers. He invited us to release judgment of our parents, even if they were "no good" parents. That was *Surrendering Judgment* 101 for me. Surrendering my judgments initiated my forgiveness process, which created a bridge to the love again.

Things had come to a head between my father and mother before I left for college. When home for a semester break, I called after months of not speaking to him and he was so excited to hear from me! That was my confirmation of a new beginning. We all start somewhere: it was my first call to *Unconditional Love*.

Much later as an adult, I received *the call* again during my training as a Spiritual Life Coach. The premise of our training was before you coach someone else you must first be able to coach yourself. This was the greatest gift to my own healing and relationship make-over with my father, because during my project I had the choice to do the work with the actual person or not.

Over the years, my father had made it clear he wouldn't re-visit old events that had wounded me; little did I know the answers were beyond him anyway. So I imagined the process in my mind's eye, journaling, speaking aloud, affirming and praying. He knew nothing of all this, and I trusted the process. It wasn't easy doing it alone because it was yet another solo thing. However, the truth is—*I was not alone!* Spirit met me at the point of my intention! I was thirsty to finally break through my own self-sabotage, which originated from the belief that I was unloved, unlovable and unloving. The ocean of truth, forgiveness and surrender quenched my thirst.

The greatest gift I gave "myself" was surrendering expectations. I loved my father and loved myself. At the same time, I knew that everything I would ever need I could have in spirit—nothing was being withheld from consciousness. In my meditations I could see my father, the little boy who had been hurt and rejected but never had the opportunity to heal. I recognized myself as a gift to him. The gifts I bore were understanding, intuition and compassion. I was able to take him off the pedestal on which I'd placed him, and end the romanticizing of what life would have been like had he been available the way I needed. Through the eyes of that little girl, I was able to see the places in me that had needed love and reassurance. And through the eyes of the woman, I was capable of loving and nurturing myself, and surrounding myself with reflections of this self-love.

It was unconditional love that became the wind beneath our wings, and commanded me to make the adjustments in my mind and heart first. It was empowering to stand on the firm ground of self-love because my mental and emotional cup was now full. I gave to my father from the overflow.

My ears became new and I heard things from him I would have missed had I still been holding on to my concept of what he "*should be*." The words we spoke became a scroll I knew I would later read when he was no longer on the planet. It didn't matter that he didn't go into great detail, because I accepted him, including his limitations.

And I had new eyes! I beheld his sensitivity, his valor, his pride and even his pain. And though he's no longer here with me physically, I look into these eyes and see him every day. I am so grateful.

My labor in earlier years gave birth to a ministry of new consciousness and transformation. I know my Dad loved me and was proud to be my father. The elders say, "Give flowers to the living." I gave my bouquet of love while he was here so I wouldn't have any regrets after he transitioned. I received more from my giving than I could have ever expected from the journey with my father. My vulnerability is the gift that keeps on giving because I'm still Daddy's Girl!

LOVE THE LIFE YOU LIVE
Anne Hartley, Australia

"I discovered that our values can be our
life purpose, our identity and a compass
for making the right choices. . ."

You know you've settled for the consolation prize when you achieve your
goals and they don't make you happy.
One day I was sitting in a plush hotel in New Zealand,
having just completed a successful tour of speaking engagements and seminars and written two very successful
books, yet all I could think about was how far removed
life was from my original plans.

I didn't know *what* I wanted, and was frustrated and
upset. Only later, when I started working with values,
did I realize that we always know what we want—only
sometimes our dreams get buried beneath a mountain
of hurt feelings and disappointments. Rather than
face another disappointment or more pain, we delude
ourselves into believing we don't know what we want. I
was no exception.

All I ever wanted from life was to have a happy marriage and healthy babies. A career was my consolation

prize for the dream never fully achieved. I didn't marry, although I did have children. My first child, Lisa, was born in 1968 when I was just twenty-one. My son Robbie was born six years later. Having children as a single mother wasn't a conscious choice on my part to rebel against society; I desperately wanted to get married—the fathers of my children didn't want to marry me.

Being a single mother in 1968 was socially unacceptable. We lived on the poverty line with barely enough money for food, until the discovery of books that changed the way I thought, which ultimately changed my life.

Inspired by the books, I decided to start my own business: a typing service. I didn't even own a typewriter but had optimism, and told everyone "I'm in the typing service business." Soon asked to type a thesis, I borrowed money from a girlfriend, rented a typewriter and worked from my kitchen table.

By 1980 my life was looking good, our financial situation was greatly improved, the children were thriving and I was happy. Three weeks before Christmas my children and I attended a birthday party where my son Robbie, aged five, slipped out onto the balcony, climbed onto the ledge to fly his paper planes and toppled over—we were five stories high. He died before the ambulance arrived.

Losing a child is like losing your heart. At first I felt numb. When the shock wore off, the pain hit with such intensity I didn't feel I could survive it. I walked round feeling as if my heart had been smashed into a million pieces. I wondered: *how am I still alive, able to function and manage my daily routine?*

On the outside, most people thought I was doing okay, considering what had happened. Inside, I thought, I don't think I'll ever be happy or experience joy again. If you choose to survive, you do—but it's a choice. Over time the pain eases until one day it's gone, but life is never the same. I learnt from my son's death that I had choices and how I allowed this event to shape my life was up to me. I chose to grow through the experience.

By this time I was in my thirties and couldn't understand how far removed my life was from my original goal of a happy marriage and children. I decided if I couldn't have a marriage and family, then I'd concentrate on raising my daughter and making money.

I returned to work in the investment industry in 1982 and within two years was offered a position setting up and running a women's investment advisory service. I presented seminars and was regularly interviewed by the media. Soon I was writing columns for major magazines and newspapers. This apparent success didn't just happen—I made it a reality by working hard, studying, meditating, saying affirmations and using visualizations to help me achieve my goals. During this time I also wrote my first book, *Financially Free,* and it became an immediate best-seller.

I was asked to speak at conferences in Australia and New Zealand and had regular spots on TV and radio—all the success I had thought would make me happy and yet it meant nothing. I wasn't chasing my dream; I'd pursued the consolation prize by actively seeking public recognition, hoping that would fill the void within me. It didn't.

Clearly, I needed to change my life. I gave up my financial planning business and started a new business. It was a financial disaster from the beginning and I lost a lot of money trying to make it work.

The next few years passed in a haze of confusion. My intentions were good, but there was still a lot I needed to learn about myself and about life. From being successful to being plagued with major money worries, I ended up taking a part-time book-keeping job because I needed the income. I went from being paid $150 an hour for a consultation (and thousands for a talk) to just $17 an hour—an incredible blow to my ego.

On the outside things appeared bleak, but this time in my life motivated me to do the work I do today. Life often presents our greatest opportunities under the guise of problems and I was aware I'd created my success before, and knew I could do it again. However, this time I wanted a formula, a step-by-step process in order to create what I wanted so that I wouldn't keep making the same mistakes. I knew there were others struggling like me, and if I could make it work for myself, I could then help others going through similar struggles.

I had a purpose. Experimenting with values, I discovered that our values can <u>be</u> our life purpose, our identity and a compass for making the right choices. I decided to divide values into two categories, which I call *being* and *having values.*

Our *<u>being values</u>* are the character traits of the ideal person we would like to be. I chose to be kind, loving and wise and these values changed my life. It's hard to make a wrong choice when you stop and think about how a wise person would act. By acting on these values consistently, we **give** to others through our daily actions.

Our *<u>having values</u>* are our emotional needs. These could include companionship, achievement, support, being valued or financial security. This is what we need to **receive** in order to be happy. When we take full responsibility for fulfilling our own needs our life changes and often other people come along to support us.

By being aware of both the need to give and receive we create balance and at the same time break the habit of reacting. The more we act on our values, the more our perceptions of what we can be, do and have begin to change, and in turn other people's perceptions of us alter. As a natural consequence, any limiting beliefs that may previously have prevented us from achieving our dreams transforms as well.

Once I began living my values, life began to flow and change for the better. I experienced synchronicity where the right people and the right opportunities seemed to appear out of the blue—because the reality is that we attract them when we're congruent.

One day a stranger rang and asked me if I'd be interested in ghostwriting a book for one of his clients, and believe me, the pay was a lot better than $17 an hour. I agreed and although this wasn't my ideal work, I enjoyed it. Out of the blue my accountant recommended me to someone else who wanted a book written. I ghost wrote three books in all and adapted two of Suze Orman's books for the Australian market. This work wasn't another consolation prize; it was a stepping stone, a short-term solution that paid good money for a skill I'd developed.

I knew without the worry of how to survive financially that I'd be able to focus on creating a business I really loved. I was always very clear about this. I changed the way I thought, spoke and acted, lived by my values and my circumstances changed.

During the first twelve months of working with my values-based process, my income quadrupled. My life today is far removed from what I originally imagined, but honestly I can say: I love my life, I feel so blessed!

You, too, can create a life you love—when you use your values as the foundation for all your choices.

THE EDGE OF THE UNIVERSE
Candy Bradshaw, Massachusetts

*"I stared at the obstacle, renamed it Challenge
and began to plan my strategy . . ."*

In the fall of 2005 I attended a retreat in Sedona, Arizona, a location well-known for its spiritual energy, and a major reason to visit was some of the energy currents within the area.

I felt the energy as soon as I left the vehicle. I looked up in panic, since I was told to expect light hiking and this was <u>not</u> light hiking—it was rock climbing, or mountain climbing, neither of which I had any experience doing. Our leader suggested we do the best we could and go up only to where we felt comfortable. I swallowed my panic and made the decision to at least start.

Not making very much progress, I inched forward, going right, then retreating, going left, retreating again, always looking upward. A boy about 12 appeared beside me, immaculately clean in a white shirt and white shorts. As mother of two boys I notice such details.

He smiled and said, "You can do it! No one has fallen off the mountain today."

I was tempted to inquire about the day before but decided I didn't want to know. "What's your name?" I asked

"Steven," he said, while pointing out a possible path. I assumed he was from the area and therefore knew the easiest route.

I followed his suggestions and began to make real upward progress. With each step my confidence increased. Relieved, I thought, *this isn't so bad; I just needed to be encouraged and pointed in the right direction.* Finally I made it to a plateau and the top was in sight. I was going to do it! As I looked up I could no longer see anything that could be identified as a path.

I pondered my final steps, Steven beside me once again. "Come this way, you can get to the top from over here."

Eagerly I followed him around a bend. What I saw caused my jaw to drop. Pure rock, straight up—it seemed to lead to infinity. "Are you kidding?" I yelled. "There's no way I can get up there. There's no incline, nothing to hold onto." To make matters worse, the rock wasn't even solid—it was split, a fissure, perhaps two rocks close together. I could look right through it, down to infinity.

I saw three options: I could move to the left and fall off the side of the mountain, I could fall backwards, back down the mountain or just fall through the crevice into infinity. I had the conscious thought that my driver's license was in my pack—a good thing—because when my dead body was found, at least my boys would know what happened, assuming that someone found the body before the coyotes did.

I looked again at the fissure and realized my body was way too big to fall through that crack. I always knew if I lived long enough these extra pounds would have their reward! I looked upward; 20 feet separated me from failure or success and I tried to console myself that I'd made it pretty far. I could be proud of the gains I had made—I'd climbed much farther than anticipated. None of this helped raise my spirits. At this moment the destination was not the journey, it was reaching the top and I had failed to reach it.

I looked at Steven. His face was beaming, aglow with the sunlight reflecting from his beautiful smile. "You can do it," he said. "Just go up."

Yes, just go up, but how? I was a victim of the mountain, my physical restrictions and my own thoughts. Refusing to leave this spot, I began to reflect on the events of the day that had led me to this point of failure. I am a student and teacher of Psicanica, a spiritual philosophy of Personal Power, a Science of the Soul. I had arisen early to read the Psicanic concepts of Cause and Effect. I thought about the various meanings of Cause: *Power, The ability to produce the desired effect, Will, Strength.* At this moment I was none of these. I was at the negative end of the Cause and Effect spectrum: *Defeat, Dependent, Denial.* Yes, I had failed but it wasn't my fault: *Avoidance of Cause and Responsibility.* Who could have expected me to climb all the way to the top?

I began to reflect on the other definitions I had studied earlier. Cause: *The ability to Decide, Think, Be proactive, Produce, Initiative, CREATE.* As I continued to reflect on Cause, I felt a positive change in my energy from that of failure to one of possibility. Responsibility: *The possibility of action, The ability to act.*

This mountain was just an opportunity for me to demonstrate Cause and Effect. I stared at the obstacle, renamed it Challenge and began to plan my strategy. I thought about the concepts of Cause and Effect: *Thought, Action, Decision, Power, Persistence.* I stared at the *Challenge.* There it was, plain as day, my opportunity. Just above me was about 3 inches of rock jutting out, not much, but enough to hold the front end of a sneaker. My eyes continued upward, another piece of rock, perhaps enough to hold on to. If I thrust off with my right leg and moved quickly enough I just might be able to pull this off—could at least get off the ground.

It was apparent I'd have to move quickly in order to remain balanced. My eyes continued up the slope: I saw the incline shifted downward. If I made it to this point I could crawl to the top. I had a plan, and the goal was once again within my reach. I counted to three and within seconds had made it to the top! Once at my destination I decided to journal for a few minutes and took a seat. I was enjoying my success, my Creator power, when I was disturbed by my own Being; that inner longing, the voiceless voice deep within. There it was, telling me—no, commanding me—to go to the edge, to push to the limit.

Terror! Fear of heights has plagued me all my life. I thought, *this can't be happening . . . to stand at the edge of a mountain and look into the vastness is just too much to ask.* My experience had catapulted from Cause to Effect, yet the voice continued.

I cursed the Universe; after everything that I had done to get to this point couldn't I have been allowed to enjoy my success? *I CAN'T DO THIS,* I cried to myself and wept silently, listening to the incessant beckoning of my own BEing, *go to the edge; there is nothing for you here, go to the edge of the Universe.* As I stared at the edge, Steven came over, still smiling, still beaming. We communicated silently as I prepared to move forward.

I stood and took two steps. Terror shot up through me so intensely I fell back and sat for a few moments to regroup. I remembered that in one of the Psicanica books a woman overcame fear by inching to the edge. With Steven by my side, coaxing my forward movement, still sitting, I inched to the edge. Every couple of inches

I stopped, gasping deeply to let air into my body, letting the fear ripple through me, allowing myself to integrate with it fully, reminding myself of the Psicanic concept: *I am Creator, the Cause of my own experience, all of it.* Eventually, my breathing became normal, the terror became manageable. I raised my eyes to look over the side. I couldn't believe what I saw.

From the edge I could look down into the canyon, could look onto nearby mountains, beauty only visible from the edge, beauty unable to be experienced from my 'safe' vantage point. I understood now why the voice had beckoned me to the edge. I had wanted to end the journey too soon, my goal too limited, the destination poorly defined.

By now the fear had been released. I stood up, looked to the sky, down into the canyon, no fear, no dizziness, no gasping. I moved to the other side to see what that edge had to offer—even more beauty. Steven came up and reminded me that it would be getting dark and had better start thinking about moving down the mountain.

"Are you going down the mountain with me?" I wanted to pay him for serving as my guide and mentor.

He laughed and said, "I'll show you a different way." He led me to the downward path and told me to start making my way; he would meet me at the bottom of the mountain, so off I went.

The descent down the mountain was nothing like the trip up; a winding path, no rocks, no fissures, no obstacles. I smiled at the hikers who easily climbed up the path as I contemplated my own ascent with its challenges, hurdles, opportunities and a very special guide named Steven. It was the Challenge that made this journey a remarkable event, a true growth experience.

From the endpoint I looked up the mountain. I could see Steven looking down. The distance was too great to see his face but I knew it was him by the white brilliance of his clothing in the setting sun. He made no move to come down the mountain. There was no way to thank him personally so I made a vow to lead others through their challenges as he had done for me.

AN UNDERCURRENT OF TRUST

Liz Kelaher, Australia

*"I didn't always know why these 'negative'
thoughts and feelings would come up when I
first began working with affirmations. . ."*

Several years ago while backpacking in Indonesia, I met a Buddhist man who ran a small ashram-like community in Central Java. I spent several months there learning about emotions—at the time I knew this was important, and every year since then I've come to understand more and more how this has helped me.

I have discovered that whenever I'm creating something new in my life there is *always* something that needs to go; the old way of being has to move out of my life so the new way can come in. I haven't always understood what that was or what was happening when the old energy was seeking escape.

In the process of leaving, this old energy comes into your consciousness in the form of "negative" thoughts and emotions, which will be directly related to the thing you are creating. For example, if you're creating more prosperity in your life, the thoughts and emotions that come up will most probably be money worries, or depressive thoughts about your ability to make money, and you might even have unexpected expenses at this time. If you're creating a healthier body, you may seem to become unhealthier and there will be "negative" thoughts and feelings surrounding that.

I didn't always know why these "negative" thoughts and feelings would come up when I first began working with affirmations. Often, I'd react to these feelings by stuffing them back down with more affirmations and visualisations, and of course the negativity would reappear later, usually with more intensity. Again I stuffed them back down with my affirmations, not knowing what else to do and they reappeared, usually in a more dramatic way. I was going round and round in circles—all with an undercurrent of fear and "out-of-control-ness."

I wasn't aware of what these events and emotions were trying to do. They were old stuff that needed to be released, and I couldn't create what I wanted until I let go of those old feelings and emotions.

Eventually a dramatic event would "explode" these stuffed down emotions all over the place. Finally, when I would recover I could move on, and the new way of being would settle in. This is a very difficult, painful, drawn-out way to create new things in life.

Well, there is another way—a better way—to deal with this.

The Buddhist man taught me about releasing feelings and it's a very simple process. Here are the steps:

1. When a strong emotion comes up, the first thing to do is to stop what you are doing and close your eyes.

2. Take a couple of deep breaths into the pit of your stomach.

3. This is really important— Let go of the thoughts surrounding the emotion, the event that caused the feeling, the idea or concept that has created the emotion in you. Don't think, feel!

4. Allow the emotion to flow though your body. Feel it, feel where it is in your body; it could be in your solar plexus, your heart area, chest or throat or anywhere else. Focus on the feeling.

5. Keep feeling it, and feeling it, and feeling it until it is no longer there, probably in about 20 seconds to 5 minutes. It could be sooner. But if the feeling is still there, keep feeling, and don't stop untill it's gone. It is very important that you do not go back to the thoughts surrounding the feelings or emotion. Stay with the feeling.

6. That's it! You may find that similar emotions will recur. Just keep going through the process whenever they recur, it just means that you have more stored inside you waiting to be released, it will eventually all be released if you follow these instructions every time.

If the emotion continues longer than a few minutes you will probably find that you are holding an idea or thought regarding the event that brought up the emotion, wanting to blame, or analyse or indulge in self-pity. Let these thoughts go. Just feel.

When a "negative" emotion surfaces I now welcome it because I know it's not negative at all, just old energy leaving so new energy, a new way of being can come into my life. This doesn't mean I don't have strong emotions, I do, but they do not overwhelm me. I know why it is there and know it will pass. There is an undercurrent of "Trust."

IT GETS DARK BEFORE YOU SEE THE STARS

Annie Miller, Australia

*"From the power of choice came energy and
from the energy came compassion. . ."*

I didn't recognize the woman standing at the kitchen sink looking out the window. In fact, I had not recognized myself for a long time. As I looked at the scalding water flowing over my hands and into the sink, the recurring chatter within continued: *I'll be happy when the air conditioning is put in, when my baby gets older so I can sleep through the night, when I can exercise more*—convincing myself that life will be better "when."

Frustration had set in. *Why do I feel so inadequate, and where does the fear and dread come from when the phone rings? Why do I feel physically ill when we're invited somewhere? Where did the intense emptiness come from, when I didn't even wish to speak to anyone? What had happened to the person I used to be who had been efficient, creative and social?* Day after day, I endured darkness and physical pain within, moving in a robotic state, barely aware of anything around me . . . only the suffocation of nothingness, the tears of everything.

It was on this very "normal" day when my life changed profoundly. I'd never realized that a "star" could shine so brightly during the daylight hours, bright enough to make me look up from burnt hands and become aware I was bathed in a light so golden it completely mesmerised me, and a sense never felt before. At that moment the realization dawned: I had the **power of choice—an option not to be unhappy**. I could choose to stay in the state I had been in for 4 years or could move on. **I had the power to change!** Unbelievable warmth flooded through me and eased my darkness.

The doors of my mind were opened, and intuition, which had been neglected in those past years, greeted me again. I felt an energy and awareness of the moment, more connected with the universe and myself than ever before. I had been presented with a gift, a gift of the present. "If you shed tears when you miss the sun, you also miss the stars." –*Stray Birds,* Tagore.

You could call this my "happiness" star: the absolute realization that happiness comes from within, that life will always be full of challenges, so it seems to be wiser and simpler to accept both and just be happy anyway. Had I overcome adversity in a moment? Had I in a heartbeat overcome the pain of heavy personal financial loss, deep postnatal depression of four years and the recent news of my closest friend's breast cancer? I believe in the darkness of despair I'd been handed one of the most important lessons in my life—given courage to face my monster. Courage to become the true me. I was not my bank account or my resumé or my neighbourhood. I was not everything I was *trying* to be and was not my mistakes. I was not seeing me as who I truly was. I was focusing on what I thought I *should* be, what I *should* look like and how I thought my life *should* be looking. I was comparing myself to others and waiting for all the tomorrows to be happy.

From the power of choice came energy, and from the energy came compassion. Compassion for others had never left me; compassion for myself had fled. Adversity may draw anyone into the depths, where fears and weaknesses live in shadows and the capacity for goodness to oneself feels trapped... I was determined not to go back.

Being kinder to myself with simple things such as smiling, really smiling at me in the mirror every morning, meditating and just "being" rather than doing, was a good beginning. Respecting my own time allowed a heightened sensitivity and wonder at nature. I began discovering sparkling beauty in many previously unnoticed things. Devouring spiritual material provided knowledge and enabled me to grow. I had a puppy-like eagerness, which became a passion.

From compassion came humour and joy... laughter at many things and joy at nothing in particular. My laughter had been silenced, and as harsh as it sounds, that had been an unwitting choice. Depression and a choice to be unhappy meant many feelings had been submerged which were now able to surface and be released one by one. We forget to play when we take life too seriously. I learned the meaning of fun all over again, and took great pleasure from spreading it to others. Life is short, light the candles, use the silver and wear your party shoes! You can't make someone happy but you can certainly affect his or her quality of life through your own good humour and kindness. It requires very little to do so much for another person. When someone we know is going through a difficult time, often we can feel overwhelmed, especially if that person is ill or needs a great deal of attention. And yet, a huge smile or an unconditional gesture such as a hug, sending a card or cooking a meal can be one of the most healing and joyous things to do . . . joyous to those who give and joyous to those who receive.

Life sets up situations for all of us that we would prefer not to be in but cannot avoid. These are part of our personal journey. How we deal with them and whether we have the courage to face them is also part of our journey. We learn from adversity not from strength. I've learned to accept sorrow, sadness and grief as feelings; to pay attention, work through them and move on. The intense pain that one feels with grief is crippling at times. Now I use my choice to be happy as well. True happiness coming from within also accepts the sadness. As Albert Camus said, "In the depths of winter I finally learned there was in me an invincible summer."

There are only few times now when I am challenged with this. My reminder: this is an opportunity for choice. How we actually live each moment is how we live our life.

My "happiness" star appeared after it had gotten very, very dark, and led me to the place where I feel freedom, love and gratitude. There are many days when I feel so empowered I could burst from this joyous choice.

Messenger from the Woods

Barbara Burke, New Jersey

*"For the first time there was a hint of
spring in the air and my spirits lifted at the
prospect of an end to the long winter. . ."*

There she was again. The half-grown deer
shuffled out of the woods and across my
back yard, heading for the area underneath
the bird feeder because the birds, in their zeal to get
the prime seed morsels, always knocked some to the
ground. Until I moved to this house I'd never realized
that deer liked bird seed, but upon second thought figured it must be because the seed was similar to the oats
we used to feed the horses my grandparents kept.

I get many deer in my yard, but this one was especially recognizable because she had a moth-eaten look.
The fur around some areas of her back was thinned
out or gone completely, while the rest looked normal.
I couldn't tell if she had some kind of skin problem
or not (do deer get psoriasis?) but it made her easy to
distinguish.

The other thing about this particular deer was that
she was always alone. She would usually come into my

yard just before or just after a herd of about five or six deer had been here. Once or twice, during the worst snowstorms when there was no bare ground to be seen, I saw her in the yard with the rest of them. But she was always separate, hanging back or in another area while the regular herd jostled each other for the prime bird feeder spot. The healthier deer seemed to ignore her. I guessed that her mother had been killed, either by a hunter or by a car, and she had been forced to fend for herself. Maybe she never learned the social complexities of deer society. Whatever the reason, my heart went out to her and I found myself putting extra seed on the ground when I thought she might show up.

This particular March day was gray but warm. For the first time there was a hint of spring in the air and my spirits lifted at the prospect of an end to the long winter. I pulled out a lawn chair and sat on my back porch to read, savoring the fresh air. After a while I saw her. I must have been downwind because she didn't appear to notice me. As she hobbled slowly across the yard, she seemed to be walking more stiffly than usual. Her back legs turned inward as if she had rickets. Her coat was even more ratty-looking than the last time I'd seen her. As she settled in to eat the seed that had fallen from the feeder, I watched her turn her head fretfully and gnaw at her back as if scratching it. Then I realized that the missing patches of hair matched the areas that she could reach with her neck. She had worn the hair on her body by repetitive scratching. I smiled sadly as I looked down at my own nails. I have a lifelong habit of biting them, and can't seem to break it even though I want to. "We're not so different, are we, sweetie?" I murmured under my breath.

The little deer took her time and scoured the ground for every last seed. I longed to go to the garage and get more, but knew she would run the second I stood up. Finally she was done. As she turned back toward the woods, she seemed to hobble more slowly than before. Head down, she seemed defeated and lonely. "You think that nobody knows you or loves you, don't you, sweetie?" I thought. "But *I* do."

Then it struck me: *that this is how God feels about us. God sees our struggle to survive, our unmet needs for love and acceptance, our self-destructive habits – and loves us despite and even because of them.* As I sent a wave of love toward my deer disappearing into the underbrush, I felt it wash back toward myself. Feeling the connectedness of all things, I whispered a prayer of thanks to the universe for creating this beautiful planet that we all share, and for the unifying power of love that connects us.

COURAGE

Naomi Blake, Australia

*"A major step was to find something I
was so passionate about I'd do whatever
it took to make it happen. . ."*

L ast night I stood up and spoke about my life. I told the group about who I used to be and who I am becoming as I explained my journey of hardships, triumphs and life lessons. They could feel my passion as I talked about what a success I felt I had become.

Does it sound easy? If you had asked me a few years ago to describe myself as a success, I would have run a mile away. I've always struggled to be able to speak convincingly in public. Yet last night I really did well – my inner critic suggests a little too fast, but my worthy self knows I did just fine.

About 4 years ago, my unhappiness became an intolerable ache. On the surface I seemed OK, yet was frustrated and dissatisfied—*stuck*. My dreams of kids and a husband were fading, and there were many reasons why this was everyone else's fault.

I changed careers, but all the same frustrations and blame kept coming up. I slowly realised I was doing a good job of sabotaging myself. Every time I had an opportunity to shine, my power deserted me. I was the common denominator in all my unhappiness.

In the way of the universe, an opportunity to transform my life appeared. These opportunities can come from anywhere—many use the work of Louise Hay, or find a great counsellor, or learn to meditate. For me it came from the enneagram - an ancient system of understanding people based on nine personality types. Each type is motivated differently by what they think they need to do to survive; we use this defence to prevent ourselves from being vulnerable, and therefore from falling in love and being our true essence.

It taught me what I'd learned as a baby. As a type nine, I was asleep to myself; in other words, I had decided not to have a personal agenda or passion, believing that my family wouldn't love me if I was too much of my own person, or if I asked for what I wanted. So it became easier not to know what I wanted. Yet ironically, I could not **be** loved until I was able to stand up for myself.

I gave as much attention to unimportant issues as to essential ones. I sought a comfortable and familiar life, to avoid the conflict associated with asking for what I wanted. No wonder people overlooked me—I was working very hard to be invisible! I drifted through life.

Getting to this awareness was very confronting! However, the many nights of tears and struggling with dormant emotions were still better than a life of "quiet desperation." I started looking forward to discomfort and anxiety, because it meant I was changing and being different.

A major step was to find something I was so passionate about I'd do whatever it took to make it happen. This would make it much easier to deal with conflict and give me the courage to change. From this point, my life became a ride on a roller coaster. I took six great months off and relaxed, learned belly dancing, and lost a lot of weight without trying. I also found my passion. Just by looking at my bookshelf, I realised I'd been buying books about the emotional connection to health since I was 19. They were all there: *Love Your Disease, It's Keeping You Healthy*; *You Can Heal Your Life*; *Love, Medicine and Miracles*. Working with the body by working with the mind felt as natural as breathing and could be the basis of my passionate life. The penny dropped: **I** wanted to be a mind/body counsellor.

I enrolled to study counselling, and became a *Heal Your Life* teacher. I was on my way! But then the money ran out, and I couldn't get a job. For the first time in my life I faced real hardship, and needed to go on un-employment benefits. What a humiliation; it was very uncomfortable.

In hindsight (the best sight there is...) this was my **real** kick start into a new way of being. As things had always come easily to me, I believed that anyone without a job was simply thinking the wrong thoughts—they must have a victim complex, or didn't really want to be successful.

I discovered there are many reasons why things don't happen. Sometimes it's simply not the right time. Sometimes learning to love yourself enough to get a job is too painful. Sometimes the universe is trying to tell you something.

What I needed was compassion. In judging others as being wrong, I was finding myself wrong. When I ignored other people's pain, it meant I could ignore my own. From this I learned empathy and kindness towards others. I opened up to the emotions that come when you stand in another's shoes, and began to really ap-preciate that we're all doing the best we can. I realised that seeing something deficient in them is neither right nor useful. And, my sense of something deficient in me is equally useless. Now, if I catch myself thinking negative thoughts about someone, or that they are wrong, I mentally kick myself in the butt and think: *remember being unemployed.*

Sometimes I just wished for the comfort of my old life, but my determination to succeed surprised me; this passion thing was really motivating!

Another big lesson came when I was finally offered a job. I was so relieved that someone wanted to employ me that I didn't ask myself if I wanted it, or listen to my internal warning bells. Simply because they asked, I thought I should take the job. Surprise, surprise, I hated it. Then, after a fortnight they fired me!

I waited to be angry, but wasn't: I had one of those 'aha' moments. I realised that really, deep down, I didn't want to work there and they'd done me a favour. I'd created my unhappiness by not trusting enough to wait for the job I *really* wanted. In starting on this journey of recognising my own worth, it has become harder to take just any job; the upside is the right job is more likely to come along.

Over the next few years I continued studying at university, struggling along on 30% of my previous wage, doing temporary jobs along the way. I then applied for my first counselling job at a prestigious organisation just for the practice of an interview, but they actually offered me the job!

About the same time I ran a *Heal Your Life* workshop, which went really well. I was able to use my professional skills with these wonderfully creative exercises. For the first time I saw my own power! This was important work I wanted to do and I was not there for the money but to make a difference.

Of course, I'd thought things would even out then, but it continues to be a roller coaster. However, I like that now. It means I'm alive and moving forward!! And achieving my goal meant I needed to look at why I wanted it in the first place. I thought once I became a counsellor life would be perfect, yet I struggled with the rules set by my new employer, and felt that familiar sense of blame towards others.

I realised it was the **process** of achieving the goal that was important. In the past I'd found it much more comfortable to think I didn't have the power (others had taken it) rather than risk standing up for myself. Now, I have proved to myself that I have the power to become what I want to be. I can't blame anyone else anymore for what's not right and I am no longer a victim.

So for the first time I decided not to run away. I confronted what I believed was making me feel powerless and moved through it. I'm not different now because I'm a counsellor; I'm different because I believe in myself and am creating a new life—building my private practice and dealing with the issues of the self-employed. I have to believe in myself; if I don't, nobody else will. I need to make darn sure people see me and hear about me through promoting my skills. I can take the risk that people may not like working with me, and know I'll survive even if they don't. One of the best aspects is my monthly newsletter, where I say to the world that this is the way I see things. I might be vulnerable to criticism (who does she think she is?) yet I love it!

So, what's inspirational about my story? Well, the fact that you, too, can do it. You *can* find something that you love enough to persevere through the hard times. I finally understand what it means to love what you're doing, and the money will come. And, in a bigger sense, you don't have to be seduced by your present limitations in anything at all. Your mind and beliefs may tell you that the way you are is all you deserve; change and risk dying. But that's an illusion as a slower death comes from not being true to the love inside. The journey is never really over—it simply becomes better placed in your life. Yes, there are challenges, but I'm driving the bus now.

In desperation before my speech I asked the affirmation cards for help. They told me, "You deserve to be loved." We all do; we all deserve to move past our fears and have love for others and ourselves. I did it; you can do it too.

LOOKING DOWN AT MY ABYSS
Michaela Herrera, New Mexico

"I was stunned and overwhelmed by the extreme
generosity from a complete stranger. . ."

The year 2002 will forever be etched in my memory as *the* most frightening and difficult year of my life. My Father died in August of 2000, and two years later, I was still deeply entangled with his estate. To say his affairs were left in disarray would be a massive understatement.

While ill, he had drained his bank accounts keeping his art gallery and his personal life afloat, not aware he was terminally ill. I suppose he thought he would recover and get things financially back on track, as he made money very easily as a sought-after accident investigator.

By the time he had exploratory surgery it was discovered that instead of the original diagnosis of *diverticulitis,* he was riddled with inoperable tumors throughout his colon. After an immense struggle in intensive care, he left this world only 16 days later. I was alone, and the sole beneficiary of a very big and complicated financial mess—his estate.

The estate had very little liquidity and was primarily a variety of assets that either no one wanted or assets coveted by people who were out to take advantage of me because of my ignorance. I won't even get into this cast of characters. I had to move very slowly to avoid foolish mistakes. The slow economy and the attack on September 11, 2001 had left many very shaky about buying luxury items.

Unable to sell these, his beautiful home had gone into foreclosure, as well as my own home; all my bills were overdue—credit card, car, electric, and more—and I spent every waking hour working to sell items, refinancing, seeking loans, and anything else I could think of to keep me and the estate afloat. No job would pay me enough to meet the amount I needed, or fast enough to save me.

By summer of 2002 I was completely backed into a corner. I had exhausted all my resources, was barely able to get up and function, nearly sleepless, overwrought, and filled with fear and pain knowing how disappointed my Father would be that I'd squandered his legacy.

I got a few really low-ball offers I could have taken and gotten out of the messes. But I would have walked away with absolutely nothing. I refused these people. I felt if I settled, I'd allow them to somehow rip off my Dad, and I couldn't bear to do it . . . just the idea struck at my heart. I felt I was looking down a very dark abyss.

I had begun sleeping on the futon in my office with the TV on, so when I woke up in the middle of the night I'd have something to distract me from the stress and intense anxiety. I had also made a poster with affirmations and put it at the foot of the futon, so it was the first thing I saw. Between endless calls and wheeling and dealing, I often ended in the fetal position on the futon, just repeating the affirmations over and over:

> *Life is safe and all that I need is always taken care of.*
> *I am a money magnet.*
> *I like money and money likes me.*
> *I now have the Midas touch.*
> *Everything I do creates a great wealth of riches for me now.*

Sometimes I'd just lie there and mumble these affirmations over and over. I'm sure if anyone had seen me they would have taken me straight to a psychiatric ward!

The date for the actual foreclosure auction of October 30th was fast approaching. I was still wheeling and dealing, and added to my affirmation repertoire, looking into the mirror every day, saying, "You are a winner!"

One day I was in Sedona clearing out the last of my Father's things from his home before resigning myself to losing it. I found myself on the phone with Glenn, an older gentleman I'd met in a restaurant with my Grandfather the year before. Glenn was about 86 years old. Gramps and I had noticed him immediately and enjoyed a delightful conversation before exchanging numbers.

We didn't really know each other. Now I look back on that call and don't even remember why I had thought to call him. I do remember explaining my situation with the house, and Glenn asked the amount I owed.

I said: "It is $16,000. I have two days before it's to go on the auction block."

He replied: "I'll pay it off and you can pay me back when it sells."

I was stunned and overwhelmed by the extreme generosity from a complete stranger. Even my own family members who had the money hadn't helped or demonstrated faith in me, and here was a man I had met only once offering to help.

He and my realtor drove to Phoenix to pay the money and filed two hours before closure. I would have lost the house, a huge bulk of the estate and all I'd worked for during two long, arduous years.

Glenn paid this money, and with the combination of his faith and mine there was an offer on the house the very next day— a good offer!

Life is brighter! Since then, I've been able to get my house out of foreclosure, credit is cleaned up, all debts paid, I've recently bought a new home and left the sad, scary memories behind. I moved into my new home on December 21st 2004, and found out later from Glenn's daughter that he died on that very day.

I will always think of him as my angel who saved me from a distressing fate. No longer am I looking down a sad abyss, but now stand on high ground looking down at Santa Fe, the city I love, enjoying the magical sunsets from my beautiful new home—once again a woman in control of my life.

After all the heartlessness and greed I experienced, it was Glenn who restored my faith in humanity and showed me there are safe people in the world who want to help others and do good things. His generosity proved the world really is a safe place, just like the affirmation says.

THE REBEL – NOT YOUR AVERAGE FAIRYTALE ROMANCE

Sharon L Horstead, Canada

*"It was so easy for me to blame the frogs
for my lonely life: if they would just open
their eyes and their hearts, then one of
them was bound to fall for me. . ."*

When I was 42, I finally found my True Love. I had been looking for him for a very long time and had even gone through some miserable periods when I'd completely given up. When he finally showed up, everything changed, and life became richer than I could have imagined. My other dreams started coming true as well. Life is now wonderful, but even though this love story has a happy ending, it isn't a fairytale where the handsome prince rescues the downtrodden princess. She rescues herself.

I was having a good life. Despite a lack of romance in my life, I was blessed with a loving family, wonderful friends, a great job and interests that I enjoyed. Although I can't say I was content, my life was far from wretched. There was, however, one dark spot. The one thing I wanted and didn't have was an intimate, loving relationship with the man of my dreams. Where *was* he, and what was taking him so long to find me? I figured I was a pretty good catch—warm, loving, smart, funny, capable, romantic, generous and ready for love. I couldn't understand why the men I dated, as few as they were, couldn't see that about me. Why didn't they think I was as great as I thought I was? What was wrong with them? Why was I getting all the frogs and no prince?

I'm currently taking a class about marketing and one question we were asked is, "If you were to go on a public rant about something you're passionate about, what would that angry outburst be?" That's a brilliant question, on many levels. I suppose it would be about personal responsibility, personal accountability. It was at the forefront of all my dreams coming true.

We've become a litigious society, looking for someone else to blame for the pain we feel, and to compensate for our losses. This is such a debilitating perspective because it casts us in the very limiting and miserable role of Victim—we give our power away when we blame external circumstances or other people for our sorrows. Accepting personal responsibility for what happens in our life, in contrast, is very liberating because it casts us in the empowered and enlightened role of Rebel. A rebel is someone who is her or his own authority, who refuses to give power to others. It was so easy for me to blame the frogs for my lonely life: if they would just open their eyes and their hearts, then one of them was bound to fall for me. As much as I believed I was doing everything possible to find my True Love, it wasn't his fault that he couldn't find me. I was responsible for being single. It was always my choice. The castle gates were closed. Of course, I didn't see it at the time.

I've studied spirituality and metaphysics for many, many years. The one thing I personally know to be true about the way that God (or whatever you choose to call That Which Created Us) works is that God gives us what we truly want. God also gives us free will and the ability to choose what we want. I couldn't understand why God wasn't helping me get the love I wanted (someone else to blame!). But God was actually giving me what I wanted, to be single.

So what changed for me? How did I end up with my sweetheart? I took responsibility for my life and made a new choice. Even though I knew in my heart and consciously thought I wanted love, I had an unconscious thought that I didn't. A friend and I were talking one day about forgiveness. I told her how a married friend had really hurt me once by saying, "Sharon, if you had a man in your life, we'd be much better friends."

I was stunned and asked, "What do you mean by that?"

She said, "Then we'd be able to do 'couples things' together."

My current friend asked why this hurt so much, and I told her it reminded me of high school. Back then, one of the main reasons I wanted a boyfriend was so I would fit in with all my other friends who had one. I remember feeling then, as with my married friend later, that I shouldn't need a man to validate who I was or to increase my worth: I should be loved and accepted just for me, for who I was as a person. I rebelled against a society that said I needed to be half of a couple rather than a whole individual. Of course I was petulant, like a three-year-old stomping her foot, not really a Rebel.

Naturally, God gave me exactly what I wanted. Every time I didn't like something that was happening in a relationship, I'd think: *I don't have to put up with this nonsense. I'm doing fine taking care of myself.* Zing! Just like a fairy godmother, God granted my wish and I got to take care of myself. With my new insights into how I was choosing to be alone, I was able to forgive my married friend. How could I not? Her kind soul was just mirroring the position I had adopted in high school so that I would have the opportunity to choose something different.

Then I became a true Rebel and chose coupledom for my own reasons, not someone else's. My new thoughts became, *I choose to have a loving relationship now, just for me, because it is what my heart wants. I choose to give and receive love and have a new experience of myself and of life.*

Zing! Two weeks later at a Christmas party, I remembered my choice, and instead of waiting on the sidelines, I went to talk with a group of three handsome men. I flirted a bit and then left, pleased I'd taken responsibility and shown God that I was ready for love, even if nothing came of this particular encounter. Oh, but it did!

One week later, I went out for 'casual coffee' with one of those gentlemen. Six hours (and a dinner) later, I was feeling very happy. On our second date, God gave me a little nudge to let me know I was on the right track. For years, I've been saying, "When I finally get married, I'm going to walk down the aisle to the great Etta James belting out that classic song, "At Last." Just as my date and I were having a conversation about how God speaks to us in the language of coincidence, guess which song played in the restaurant! My prince didn't have to slay any dragons or scale any cliffs to get me. I simply let down the drawbridge and welcomed him in. Now I have the love that my heart has always longed for.

I mentioned that since finding my True Love, all my other dreams have started to come true. That's because I have truly become a Rebel. I am the authority of my life, make my own choices and take responsibility for what happens to me rather than blaming someone else (okay, at first thought, it's sometimes still tempting to put it on someone else.) When things aren't going the way I'd like them to, I now check in to see what messages I'm sending to God about what I want. When my thoughts are in alignment with my heart, that which I desire comes to me in wonderful ways, and I say thank you to my fairy godmother . . . I mean, God.

Animals as Angels

Stephanie Swink, RScP, California

"Would I get the sign I'd asked for?"

Have you ever considered the backwards spelling of "God?" Go ahead try it! If you have been blessed enough to share a bond with these amazing creatures you might understand why it makes perfect sense that the Divine and the Canine share the letters in their name.

Animals of all types, wild and domesticated, have always been a magical and sure-fire way for me to recognize the Divine in form. I've been fortunate enough to share my life with all kinds of creatures from dogs, cats, birds, reptiles, fish, and rodents, to goats, chickens, horses and the occasional wild rescue. These animals were an integral part of my family and childhood, and continue to be a constant source of companionship and joy throughout my adult life. But as it often is with relationships in our lives, and try as we might not to compare, some souls seem to shine differently and brighter in our hearts and memories. Such is true for a golden fur angel by the name of Jazzmin.

Jazzy was a yellow Labrador Retriever who filled my heart and melted literally thousands of others in the 14 years she graced my side. But as you will discover as you read on, her support and devotion did not end with her physical existence.

From work to school to church, Jazzy went everywhere with me and had a huge fan base. She opened many hearts as a volunteer "Pet Encounter Therapy" dog for institutionalized youth and hospitalized elderly. And since she attended every class for two years (and snored loudly through our "silent" meditations), it was even suggested she don a doggie cap and gown for our graduation as spiritual counselors!

After nearly eleven years of endless energy, Jazzy slowed down. She lingered in her old age for one obvious reason—I needed her, and she knew it. Always the unconditional loving companion, she pushed through the feebleness and health problems to continue to be my one constant and unwavering friend. Eventually, with the supportive guidance of an animal loving minister, I faced the agonizing truth that my friend was suffering and might indeed need my help beyond the weekly chiropractic and vet appointments.

So in the way I'd learned to speak with animals through mental pictures as well as spoken words, I let her know how much I loved and appreciated her; that I did not want her to suffer and hold on for me. I told her if she needed to go I would understand and would be all right. Then I asked her to let me know in obvious ways if she needed me to help her on her way. Two days later, the dog fondly known as "the sow" due to her voracious eating habits, did what she had never done in 14 years and stopped eating. Helping her through her transition was by far the most difficult thing I have ever done in my entire life. She was the closest thing I have had to a child. So when she rested her big golden head on my lap and took her last breath, my grief was beyond description; only the loss of my human best friend two years before compared. Kathleen Barnett, whose nickname was Barnie, had died tragically and mysteriously on her 27th birthday leaving a four-month old baby girl and a 5- year old daughter. And now I'd lost my other best friend. I was devastated and felt crushingly alone. The only thing that pierced my grief stricken world that day was something my sister said as we stood at the grave in my Mother's yard. She shared a feeling that Jazzy was "on the other side" with Barnie; and without understanding why, I heard her words and felt just the slightest bit better.

The next afternoon, with the cloud of missing Jazzy hanging heavily over all of us, I picked up a catalog magazine and mindlessly thumbed through it. It fell open to, of all things, an advertisement of pet memorial frames to place your pets picture, a poem and name in. I stared at it for several moments before recognizing the incredible tri-level synchronicity of what I was looking at. The example of the poem was the one read by the veterinarian as Jazzy passed, the picture was of a yellow Labrador, and the dogs name in the ad... Barnie! I broke out in chills (I like to call them "God Bumps") and KNEW that Jazzy and Barnie were not only together but with me in Spirit at that very moment.

The next day I left San Diego and my family to return to Orange County, where I'd moved two years before. I knew I had to face very pressing issues of finding a new home and job, or giving it all up and returning to San Diego. I decided to ask my newest angel, Jazzy, and her ethereal companion, Barnie, to help guide me in what to do at this turning point in my life. Soon after, as I was driving and contemplating the nature of my "angel team", my cell phone rang and startled me. I smiled, wondering if this was the sign. Little did I know just how obviously this angelic duo had chosen to support me! A series of amazing events and opportunities transpired from that call and literally within hours I had a dreamy place to live as well as a perfect new job!

Months passed and I began to visit shelters and rescue organizations to find my next canine companion. Much to everyone's surprise, as well as my own, I did not come home with the first dog I met, or the second or third. I needed to feel something, a special kind of connection. More months passed, I upped my search and still nothing. Finally, on a misty morning when I felt particularly lonely for Jazzy the thought occurred to me to ask her for help. After all, hadn't she and Barnie proven to me they were readily available? So I closed my eyes and pictured my two best friends in my mind, asking them for support in finding my next perfect dog; specifically requesting they make it obvious. I needed a sign to know if it was right. I felt sure they would oblige and felt excited and hopeful.

Not long after that prayerful morning my boyfriend North spontaneously suggested we visit the shelter. As we walked in, a volunteer locked the gate behind us to close for the day. "Take your time!" she said. As we passed the familiar sad faces of so many sweethearts looking for homes my heart ached to save them all. We rounded the corner to face what appeared to be an empty cage. There was no hanging paperwork file. Suddenly out of the shadows bounded a smallish shaggy gray dog with black ears, muzzle and tail. He had large brown light filled eyes and THE cutest face filled with the most obvious and genuine doggy smile! Unlike the other dogs traumatized by their surroundings, this little guy engaged with us immediately, tail wagging like a propeller and a kiss for good measure. I was smitten!

"There is no information on his cage yet" we were told, "because he was found wandering the street and brought in only about five minutes ago. You can fill out an application and if no one claims him you'll be in the running to adopt him. But he will go fast, adorable dogs that size never stay here long." As I filled out the paperwork I wondered where he came from, if he'd be claimed and if he was "the one". Would I get the sign I'd asked for?

The volunteer reached for the clipboard and suddenly I realized something was missing. "Whoops! Hold on," I said. "How do I identify which dog that application is for?" She took her pen and smiled as she said, "Oh, we already gave him a name as soon as he came in. It just fit him." Her pen scratched on the top of the form six letters… "We call him *Barnie*." Speechless and in awe I turned to North as tears began to blur my vision. He beamed at me and pointed at his arm as he raised it. All the hair stood on end (more "God-Bumps!"). He put his other arm around my waist and quietly said, "Love, I think you just found your dog."

He was right of course. Barnie and I have developed a relationship in our three years to stand proudly next to my precious golden girl. He delights family and strangers alike with his intelligent and humorous antics. And the healing magic of his name has helped me come to terms with the loss of my human pal as well. I often feel I've been given an angel in fur form.

As for my angelic dynamic duo… they continue to delight and inspire me and I am so grateful. Sometimes I imagine the raucous sounds of barks, laughter, howls, and squeals of delight that will ensue when we all reunite on the other side of the veil. What a party! Don't be surprised if you hear it!

MY LIFE-CHANGING DECISION

Sharlene Bauer, California

"When I became absolutely quiet and calm, I knew the answer was within me, from my deepest knowing.. . ."

I divorced when my son, Christopher, was about three and a half years old. Within a year, I fell in love and moved to New York to remarry. I sent Christopher to California every summer and over the Christmas holiday to visit his father, stepmother, half-brothers, and half-sister. While he was away, I checked how he was doing by regular telephone calls, mostly by speaking with his stepmother who liked to talk.

While attending my niece's birthday party in California many years later, my former husband pulled me aside and said, "Chris wants to live with me now, but he's afraid to tell you." I was shocked and upset by this surprising news.

"I'll think about it," I said. For weeks afterward, thoughts continually raced through my mind: *I am the better parent for Christopher. I have done so much for him in the decade he has been living in our blended family with a stepfather and three older stepsisters. How could he spring this on me?*

I loved Christopher very much, for he brought a special joy to my life. How could I bear not having him near me as part of my daily life? I felt guilty I hadn't realized that my moving to New York had begun to affect him. The question replayed in my head during every action of my day: What should I do? My main purpose in life was to raise him, to care for him, to be sure he was healthy, happy and doing well in school. I remember the tears that slid from the edges of my eyes during yoga class as I struggled to discover the right answer.

I decided to attend a weekend retreat at Kripalu Center for Yoga and Health in Lenox, Massachusetts, known for its beautiful, peaceful surroundings, scrumptious vegetarian meals, yoga, and meditation. I arranged a Rest & Relaxation weekend with my husband, Ralph, during the Christmas holiday when Christopher was in California. The retreat schedule consisted of early morning yoga, then a buffet of delicious breakfast foods, free time for a walk, reading, or massage. The evening program of enchanting music and meditation brought me to a wonderful place of peace inside.

The second day during the morning yoga I felt stiff. The room seemed gloomy, for the sun had not risen and the skylight windows remained dark. I enjoyed breakfast, but suffered a slight headache from drinking twig tea that lacked the caffeine to which I was accustomed.

On the day before we left for our suburban home in Long Island, Ralph and I bundled up to take a walk around the retreat's expansive grounds. Fresh snow had blanketed the landscape. It frosted the bushes and tree branches and nearly obscured the lakeside path we followed. We breathed deeply; the cold, crisp New England air smelled of pines. As I lagged behind Ralph, I remember hearing my footsteps crunch, breaking the silence of our borrowed world. I absorbed the serenity and thought about nothing at all.

Suddenly the answer popped into my head and calmness and peace replaced the turmoil in my heart. In the days following my revelation, the issue became more and more clear. It was not about what was right for me, and neither was it about repayment for all I had done for him. My son wanted and needed to be physically and emotionally closer to his father, and if I said "No," it could certainly damage Chris's relationship with me.

At home, I pondered, "Where did the answer come from?" I believe the beautiful, tranquil surroundings of Kripalu, the peaceful yoga practice, deep meditation, and nutritious food led me to a quiet place inside myself. When I became absolutely quiet and calm, I knew the answer was within me, from my deepest "knowing."

I later employed the same technique for finding answers to problems at work by allowing myself time to "get the answer" in a similar way. I learned I could simply tell my co-workers, "I'll let you know when I know." This worked well if the question or issue didn't require an immediate response.

In the summer of Christopher's fourteenth year, he went to live with his father and his family in California. I remained in New York for one year in case he decided he didn't like it. To my surprise, he enjoyed California and performed well in school. One year later, I moved to the same city and lived just three miles away. I became part of his life again and he later lived with me for a couple of years during high school and college.

Christopher is now married to a lovely woman; they have one daughter. Like his father, he is in law enforcement, and is having a successful career. He's happy and enjoys his relationship with all the members of his extended family.

I am discovering my second career and beginning to fulfill what I believe is my life purpose: helping people improve their communication skills, their understanding of each other, and ultimately promoting unity and peace in the world.

FORGIVENESS IS A CHOICE
Kathryn Juric, New Jersey

*"Immediately after letting go mentally, I
had a rush of new energy to accomplish
things I had always wanted to do. . ."*

Throughout life each of us is dealt our own *unique* deck of challenges. Like it or not, the deck is ours to face. Even from our most painful experiences, we are certain to find a lesson learned with a positive impact. Most often, we become aware of the lesson later, because it's difficult to imagine there is something positive at the time of the challenge.

One of the biggest life lessons I've learned involves the importance of forgiveness and letting go of the past, including forgiving others and **forgiving myself** in order to reach closure and achieve complete freedom to move on.

During my early adult life, my deck of cards included facing the death of my husband. He died at the young age of 34 after a very tough seven-year battle with cancer. The battle was lost following multiple chemotherapy protocols, radiation treatments, and two failed bone marrow transplants. For years, I worked on letting go of the pain and grief experienced through his suffering and death. I believe the loss of a loved one is by far one of the most difficult challenges any person faces in life because it is utterly final. There is no going back. There's no longer an opportunity to change the things that weren't said or done as well as say or do things you wish you had. In my case, all the *woulda's, coulda's* and *shoulda's* filled the background of my thoughts for years. "What if I would have done that, would he have survived? Why did I say those things? I could have been there more." I later realized these thoughts held me back from moving on.

If asked, my friends and co-workers would say I had my life together. After my husband's death, I went back to school and completed my MBA, advancing my career in corporate America. I lived in beautiful surroundings, was physically healthy and on the surface, all looked well. No one would suspect that my own "records and stories" played and replayed deep inside my mind. I didn't fully realize how these thoughts were holding me back from being completely at peace and pursuing all my dreams.

Almost a decade after my husband's death, I was single and the "woulda, coulda, shoulda" records continued to play loudly in my mind for no one to hear but me. In an effort to find complete peace, I searched and asked myself, "What is holding me back from truly letting go of the painful past? Why am I resistant to being *completely* open to receiving and giving love?" A seminar leader triggered a simple insight that had a major impact on my life: I had not fully let go of the painful past because I needed to forgive my husband and I needed to **forgive myself** of all regrets.

The realization that I needed to forgive, <u>especially</u> forgive myself was the first step I needed to take. My understanding of forgiveness, in the past, typically involved forgiving others. I never thought about the importance of forgiving myself. I had reached a point of willingness to try anything and in that moment **chose** forgiveness. At a recent workshop, I learned about the simple but powerful technique of writing a letter to help reach closure. New knowledge produces results only when action is taken to implement that knowledge. In my case, my action was to write a letter to my husband forgiving him and forgiving myself. Here is my letter:

Dear Damir,

I want you to know that I will always love you and I will never forget you, for you were my first love and we went through so much together. I will always remember the good times and the good things you brought and taught me. You were so strong and courageous to the very end. I wish you didn't have to suffer so much. I can't believe 9 years have already passed. It is now time for me to move on from the pain and suffering of your death.

Please forgive me for any action taken or word said that hurt you in any way. I did the best I could at that time. I also forgive you for everything you did or said that hurt me. I know you did the best you could at that time. We both made mistakes but in the end we both grew together and we loved each other very much.

Many times, I have reflected and questioned if I could have or should have done more to help you. But I now know I gave everything I had at that time. I realize I did not move on because I felt guilty that I could have been there more for you at the end and somehow didn't deserve to move on. I also felt by putting your suffering in the past, somehow I would disrespect your life and suffering. I now know I can move on, while always keeping you in my heart.

I release all negative thoughts, images, feelings, interpretations, and memories from the past, and, from here on, I will have only positive memories about our time together. I am inventing a new possibility for my life, the possibility of being completely open to receiving and giving of love. I release you to be free and at peace and I release myself to be free and at peace.

We are now complete. You are a wonderful, beautiful soul and I will always love you.

Love,

Kathryn

I cried deeply writing this letter. I read it over and over again and cried over and over again, then read it to a couple of friends several times and cried each time. After a dozen or so readings, I read the letter to my best friend, and realized I had FINALLY let go of the mental pain, because, during this last reading, there were no more tears and I felt at peace! I couldn't believe there were no more tears! In forgiving the past, I finally felt free: free to create many more good things in my life. I felt complete and now had a clean slate!

Immediately after letting go mentally, I had a rush of new energy to accomplish things I had always wanted to do, to reach out to people I had avoided, and to clear out any clutter in my physical environment. I had been holding onto my husband's medical bills (going back 15 years!) along with several other miscellaneous items, such as his trench coat, favorite suit, and pictures of him getting treatment. Every time I saw these things I was reminded of pain. To complete my healing, I decided to go through a complete physical purge of anything and everything that produced a negative thought. I tossed and tossed and tossed. At moments it was overwhelming but I kept thinking about the goal of complete peace and freedom. I would hold the positive memories and pictures but everything else was tossed out to open the way for new, good things to fill my life.

After I forgave myself and let go of the past mentally **and** physically, new and extremely positive things began flowing my way and have continued every day. I'm now in the process of moving to my brand new condo on the ocean (a dream come true), I have a terrific man in my life who is my best friend (the healthiest relationship I have ever had), am receiving an extra bonus from work (more than ever before), I've met new people who have led me to fresh connections and new life goals, and I am at peace with the relationships in my life!

If you have events or pain (regret, guilt, anger, sadness, hurt, resentment) from the past that might be holding you back from flowing freely in the present, I highly recommend proactively taking time and making the choice to forgive the people that hurt you and to remember to forgive yourself. In so doing, you will let go of pain, reach closure, and be free with a clean slate to create new positive things. It may be scary to let go and free up mental and physical space in life, because of the uncertainty about what will fill the openness. However, in choosing forgiveness—the rewards will be peace of mind, freedom to move on, and the ability to create new things. As so wisely stated by Paul Boese, "Forgiveness doesn't change the past, but it does enlarge the future." So choose forgiveness and take the steps—you will be amazed at what awesome new things will flow your way!

MY MIND'S EYE

Erica Ashforth, Nevada

"Trusting the process, I just let it unfold in my mind. . ."

Over the years on my quest for healing and personal growth I've come across many different methods and useful tools. The most powerful tool I have used is visualization.

The most profound experience I've ever had in life was using visualization to create the perfect home for my children and myself. I had recently moved from Portland, Oregon to central California. My children remained in Portland to finish out the school year while I got settled into my new job and found a place to live before moving them. I spent several months traveling between Roseville and Tracy, California working as an outside loan broker.

Unsure of where I wanted to settle, I spent most of my time house-sitting for a couple of different friends. I knew by summer I'd need to be settled in one place and decided on the city of Stockton. I loved the area around Victory Park and the houses there were old, charming, and just the style I loved. I knew I'd need at least two bedrooms and wanted to be within walking distance of the park. So every night before going to sleep I began to visualize living in a two-bedroom house and walking each day to the park to sit and read by the pond. In the beginning, I didn't have a clear picture of what the house looked like; however, my intention was very clear. As time went on I began to get a clearer picture of the house, the color, the layout and so on. Trusting the process I just let it unfold in my mind.

One day I was talking with a colleague who asked when I was going to settle down in one place. I told him I wanted to live in Stockton near Victory Park and needed a two bedroom house. Time went on and every night without fail I let the picture of the house I wanted become clearer and clearer in my mind's eye. A few weeks after I had the conversation with my colleague I ran into him and he informed me that he knew a house I might be interested in. He told me his father had been renting out his grandmother's old house near Victory Park and the renters unexpectedly had to move out of the state. I was very interested and he told me he would get back to me to let me know when I could go look at it.

When he called back he said, "Unfortunately, my father has decided to sell the house."

I was disappointed, but trusted that if I continued to visualize and kept my intention clear, the universe would work it all out as it was meant to. About a week passed when I heard from him again. He said he had been trying to reach me to let me know his father now unexpectedly had to go to Canada and was not going to have time to get the house ready to put on the market to sell. "If you're still interested in renting the house, go by and see it."

I remember my anxiety as he gave the directions. "Take a right on Acacia by Victory Park, go two blocks and it's a little white house on the right hand side."

I recall becoming even more anxious as I asked him if the house had brown trim. "Yes, "he said.

I continued, "Is the driveway on the left side of it?" Again he said yes, and I sensed he was becoming a bit bewildered by my questions. Finally I asked if the two bedrooms were on the right side and he paused. There was silence for a moment before he finally responded, "Erica, have you already seen this house?"

I <u>had</u> seen it—it was the house I'd been visualizing for almost two months but I felt awkward telling him how I knew such exact details. "Kind of—just tell your father I'll take it."

When I went by later that afternoon I was overcome with awe and gratitude. I felt God and the universe had heard my wish and had provided me with exactly what I wanted and more. Not only was the rent lower than I was willing to pay, the house was larger than I had visualized and had a beautiful backyard with an assortment of fruit trees for us to enjoy.

I keep a picture of this house on my desk as a reminder of what is possible to create. Visualization as a tool for healing and manifesting is something I continue to use and highly recommend to everyone. This experience showed me just how responsible I am for creating my life and how anything is truly possible.

A Journey of Love and Wisdom

Yvonne Vernon, Canada

"As I lay down again the entire
experience re-occurred, and this time I
knew the angels were there. . ."

In my forties, becoming a spiritual seeker surfaced strongly and probed my thoughts more and more until one day I asked the universe, "Is this all there is?" My spiritual journey began although I didn't know it in that moment.

When I awakened to this journey, one spiritual door after another started to open. My soul yearned to recognize the voyage, and outside pursuits have nourished it from every area of my life: relationships, jobs, marriage, family, financial, religious, emotional, and physical.

The key to getting answers: ask questions and request help when needed! The welcomed intervention of God's angels and universal assistance in this most glorious journey is close at hand. I say 'welcomed' because they cannot interfere with our free will, our God-given gift. When we use our free will and ask . . . well, watch out, because miracles start to happen.

I had asked for more time to pursue my spiritual interests. I wanted and needed time to become fully involved in facilitating Angel workshops and completing my book, but found it difficult to blend my newfound spiritual path with a busy everyday life. I could only tap into it fully when the day-to-day chores were completed and I was able to find quiet time, even if that meant less sleep. I also wanted more time with my supportive husband and teenage daughter.

There was a year left before I'd be able to retire from my job of 28 years. While on vacation with my family, a call from our personnel office informed me our branch was downsizing; since I had substantial seniority, they offered an early retirement without a pension penalty. If I accepted the offer I'd be paid a year's salary which would take me to my pension date. I could hardly believe what I heard! Of course I took it!

Depending on one's need for spiritual development we are all led in many directions and to many sources of enlightenment. We're always given what we need. In my journal entries something changed: I was able to communicate with something deep inside me and discovered if I asked a question in thought form, I would receive an answer in thought form. I sensed the presence of Angels waiting to help and the Universe waiting to help. Answers flowed easily. Sometimes there wasn't an answer to a specific question; instead knowledge was given to help answer questions which, strangely enough, surfaced later.

The writings seemed to focus on not fearing to ask for help and not doubting that it will be given if it's for my greater good. I was also told that God never gives us more than we can handle, but if we think it is more, then ask for help again for the strength to get through it. Most important: be grateful and know the request has been heard.

This brings me to share my most profound experience in healing through prayer, creating positive affirmations and rebuking negative thinking. I learned we are in control and possess all the power to utilize all that is available to us, not just from worldly resources but from supernatural resources. I also learned never to fear asking, and the importance of releasing all doubt. Faith is belief in something you cannot see and knowing it exists. Through practicing meditation and affirmations, faith builds inside us and becomes truth.

In spring of 2004 I suddenly fell ill. An ultrasound diagnosed a ureter closure, a muscular duct taking urine from a kidney to the bladder. I underwent a stent placement to open the ureter, experiencing much discomfort. A few months later, a CT scan revealed retroperitoneal fibrosis (a very rare condition and rarer in women), as well as lymphoma, secondary in the diagnosis. At the time I wasn't informed about the possibility of lymphoma, however exploratory surgery was strongly recommended in a couple of months after the stent placement healed.

Fearful, I requested another CT scan before surgery, 'in case' things had changed. Well, things *had* changed. The fibrosis had decreased significantly but a cyst had now appeared on my spleen and despite the stent, the ureter was closing more. Plus, lymphoma was now the primary diagnosis.

I asked, "What lymphoma?" The doctor finally informed me about that part of the opinion, and I refused to accept the diagnosis as truth! I prayed and claimed God's word, but must admit that doubts always came to mind as I became more emotional about this diagnosis. I started doubting my spiritual growth and the journals with angels, now convinced it all was in my head. Affirmations were becoming a blur, and soon total disbelief absorbed body, mind and spirit—although I prayed through fear and desperation. I may have been begging.

After about a month, I let go and stopped struggling during prayer . . . quit trying to control everything and asked for supernatural help, giving myself over to God completely in faith. Somehow, from that point on I breathed easier.

I changed doctors, and after meeting with two teams of oncologists, exploratory surgery was scheduled for January 2005. There was a possibility of a total abdominal hysterectomy, removal of the spleen, removal of one kidney and treatment for lymphoma to follow if the biopsy was positive. The specialists were very interested because all my tests had come back normal, despite the ureter closing more, and now I didn't fit the lymphoma diagnosis since no symptoms were evident.

I knew something positive was developing, especially my outlook. One day I came across a spiritual program about faith. The speaker's words got my attention, "There's nothing normal about being a Christian. So you hear voices? You're one of those people who believe in angels?" He continued about the lesson of faith, and his message went straight to my heart as I broke into tears. It was as if God was talking to me through the speaker.

The evening before surgery, I closed my eyes and a light so bright appeared I had to open them. I sat up and looked around to see a room full of mist. Outside illumination cast a dim light and I could see within the room but couldn't understand the mist, which disappeared. As I lay down again the entire experience re-occurred, and this time I knew angels were there, then felt calm and knew all would be well. I slept soundly. That calmness stayed with me for the entire day of my surgery.

The happiest news: no lymphoma! The surgeon had called in another surgeon, a urologist, who was able to remove the fibrosis, saving my kidney. A spleen specialist observed the cyst on the spleen and found it to be normal. A hysterectomy wasn't necessary, although one ovary was removed because the fibrosis was wrapped around it.

During my four-day stay, 300 shots of intravenous, self-administered painkiller were made available. I used only 16 in the first two days, approximately 6% of what was allowed. On the third, they removed the intravenous and gave only Tylenol.

An assistant to the gynecologist who had been in the operating room came to check on me, and I asked him if he had ever seen retroperitoneal fibrosis during his studies. He said he had not—it was very rare.

I said, "Perhaps this is why I got it, so I could gift you with the knowledge and you can help others in your career." He looked at me and laughed, then touched my shoulder as he bent forward and said, "You have gifted more people in this profession than you could imagine."

There is an endless existence of angelic and universal love. You are watched closely while on your path here and help is always standing by. When burdens become unbearable just ask and have faith.

I am so thankful that God provided healing not only for my body but my mind and spirit too. Is there more to ask for? The angels replied, "*Everything!*"

THE GIFT OF AMSTERDAM WEATHER

Feza Karakas, Turkey

*"My mind was full of unquestioned
negative thoughts and beliefs that were
sabotaging the quality of my life. . . "*

They told me my name is Feza. They told me I am a woman. They told me I am Turkish. They told me I am a Muslim. They told me I should be a good girl, be successful, make a lot of money, be reasonable, be nice to other people, not talk too much, don't ask for too much, money destroys happiness, money is bad, don't spend too much, money is security, get a good education, have a career, get married, have kids, obey the rules of society, and don't get angry. *And I believed them.*

I did my best to be what they told me I should be. I did whatever I thought I *had* to do to be happy. I had a good education, a wonderful family, a good marriage, money; I owned several small businesses that brought a secure income. I had a loving husband with an excellent career who earned a lot of money. I had two beautiful children, a girl and a boy. I had the opportunity to travel almost everywhere around the world. I thought I was my name, sex, nationality, religion, occupation, wealth, prestige, pride, and reputation.

This summarizes how I lived my life until November 1997.

In 1997 my family and I lived in The Netherlands because of my husband's job. During the first six months there I became increasingly depressed. Holland's miserable climate of rain, freezing cold temperatures and constant grey skies were affecting my happiness and kept me stuck at home, bored. One evening, feeling especially down, I started crying in front of my daughter, Idil, who was 17. Concerned, she asked what was wrong. My answer was, "I am not happy here in Holland. I'm so depressed. I hate the weather and wish I were in Turkey in the sun right now."

She tried to convince me that everything was going to be OK and I was just going through a phase. I didn't feel any better and kept on crying until Idil said something which affected the rest of my life: "OK then, how about this: imagine yourself being happy being depressed. You should enjoy your time being depressed and take full advantage of it, since it doesn't happen all the time. Two times two equals four and you want it to be five. You can't change the weather, but you *can* change the meaning you give to it. Then your depression will go away."

My daughter reminded me I had everything most people would die for, yet still wasn't happy. At that moment, I realised I only had one life to live and wasn't making the most of it. She was right . . . and it was a turning point in my life.

I began a long and deep search for what was absent. After many years of reading and going to transformational workshops, I discovered I was missing *my purpose* and the *power* to create the life I wanted, because my mind was full of *unquestioned* negative thoughts and beliefs that were sabotaging the quality of my life. One was: *I'm not good enough and don't deserve happiness.* As long as I believed the negativity was reality, I was constantly recreating stories full of fear and terror. I was at war with myself and the world.

My mind was creating everything. After taking the *Heal Your Life* workshop leader training, I discovered core negative beliefs from my past. The most powerful negative thoughts were:

> I am not good enough
> I don't deserve happiness
> I don't deserve success
> I cannot do it
> I am not lovable
> I cannot trust the world
> I am bad

I began practising meditation, and started to notice and acknowledge thoughts more carefully. I now question them and ask myself if the story I create is true or not. If the thought is negative and causes stress in my life, I change it and affirm a positive thought.

A recent situation tested if I had truly changed my thoughts, and therefore attitude. On route from a seminar in Los Angeles, I decided to visit my son and daughter in England and then fly back to Turkey. Originally, I was going to stay with my daughter Idil at her boyfriend's apartment, but he had guests visiting at the same time, so she phoned my son Berke to double-check and see if it was OK if we stayed for five nights with him. I could only hear my daughter's side of the conversation, and she was saying "It's the first time she's visiting you since you've been in England. What do you mean your girlfriend might be uncomfortable?" Hearing this,

I automatically felt hurt and believed I was unwelcome at my son's apartment.

She put down the phone and said, "Berke has to speak to his girlfriend and will call us back." I began crying and my mind filled with angry, hurtful thoughts which created a story in my mind: *my son doesn't love me any more, his girlfriend is more important to him, he's selfish and doesn't appreciate what I do for him. I'm unwanted.*

In anger I told Idil I didn't want to visit him. She was creating the same story and angrily called her brother selfish and accused him of treating me badly and unfairly.

I stopped and began questioning my thoughts: *Were they true? Could I absolutely know that they were true? Could I absolutely know that my son didn't love me and want me in his home? No, I couldn't know if they were true. I know he loves me. I know I am wanted. I know he isn't selfish. I know I haven't lost him to his girlfriend. I know he loves both of us.*

When Berke phoned back he immediately explained I was more than welcome to stay with him. I asked, "Please tell me truthfully how long you and your girlfriend want me to stay."

He said, "Until Friday, and then I'll find a hotel nearby if you and Idil want to stay longer. You're welcome in my home, and we're both looking forward to seeing you."

The questioning of my thoughts and the story I had first assumed to be true led me to avoid a hurtful and complicated situation, and instead created a pleasant, enjoyable weekend. The first was an automatic reaction, which was going to create sadness and pain; the second led to a wonderful time with my son and his girlfriend.

I now regularly take time to reflect on what has been happening in my life. This gives me a chance to pull back and view it more objectively. Through meditation and the process of noticing and questioning thoughts and affirming what I want to manifest, I reconnect with the bigger picture of who I am and what I'm doing in my journey.

I am so thankful and grateful to have the power to create the life of my dreams!

A FIRM TRUTH
Anita Stapleton-Mirolo, Ireland

*"A few months ago, I left my 'safe' office
job to pursue a career in healing. . ."*

The Greek philosopher, Plato, believed that learning is about uncovering information that we already hold deep inside us. We obtain our knowledge through "recollection" of what was known before we were born. This knowledge is truth. At first, when I was introduced to this theory, I found it a little odd and was unconvinced; however, as my life continues to unfold, it now seems to me that Plato may have been correct. Over the years, I have enthusiastically explored various avenues in an attempt to uncover the truth about life. Questions intrigued me: why are we here? and what is the secret to happiness and health? My testing of the waters on what constitutes real truth began as a child and started with the knowledge that affirmations can really change your life.

The incredible power of affirmations was revealed to me when I was about ten years old. My mother had a keen interest in yoga and meditation and she used to practice and read a lot about these areas regularly while my brother and I were at school. One day she explained to us: "It's possible for us to get what we want by using our minds. Just before we go to sleep and again first thing in the morning, if we repeat a wish about thirty times while focusing on already having it, then our wish can come true." For some reason, this information resonated with me immediately and I felt thrilled about what I could do with this knowledge.

There was a raffle to be held at my school in Dublin. Having never won anything before, I decided that this time I was going to win a prize by using my mind. After purchasing two tickets, for the next few weeks every night when I went to bed, I repeated the phrase into my pillow: "I have won a prize in the raffle at school." It wasn't difficult. Soon, it became second nature for me to carry out this affirmation every time I went to bed. I remember my feelings about the raffle beginning to change over those weeks as my confidence in the belief that I would win grew. By the time the names of the prize-winners were to be revealed, the job was carried out so well that I just expected my name to be called out. It was an incredible surreal feeling when my name was in fact announced and I walked down the school corridor to collect my prize. I recall feeling both shocked and delighted that I had created this reality. The following year, I used the same technique to get the lead part in the nativity play the school was holding at Christmas. The day the drama teacher chose me to play the part of Holy Mary was inwardly both momentous and bizarre. The sheer delight in knowing that I had once again purposefully created my future was better than getting the part itself.

In my middle twenties, I was remembering an average of three long dreams every night and was intent on knowing what they symbolised. Research into Freud

and Jung was of no help. As luck would have it (or law
of attraction in action!) I met a person who was about
to hold a dream interpretation course. Not only did the
interpretations of my dreams during these classes make
perfect sense for my life at that time, but the course also
introduced me to a whole new realm of ideas relating
to the spirit world and why we are here. Even though
these ideas were strange, I felt that they represented the
truth. In hindsight, this was a very significant course as
it steered my life journey in a different exciting direction. One evening, a fellow student mentioned a book
she said was written by a great lady who describes the
link between our particular illness and the emotional
reasons for it. I was instantly fascinated by this idea, but
couldn't remember the name of the book or author in
order to search for it afterwards.

Approximately five years later, I was practising meditation often enough, knowing and understanding that
life takes care of itself, knowing that the present moment
was the best place to be and harnessing the wonderful
power of creative visualisation. All along, I knew that
affirmations worked, however had stopped doing them
and had never really understood *why* they worked. Recently I was introduced to the philosophy of Louise Hay.
When I read *You Can Heal Your Life* in 2004, in a way it
was like a coming home. She wrote about many things
I knew and loved to read about, such as how we create
our own reality, but more importantly it clearly explained
how affirmations worked. Of course, I realised then that
this was the book I had been told about on the dream
interpretation course that had interested me so much
before. This book is now my bible.

"Loving yourself," Louise Hay says, "causes tiny
miracles to happen." Focusing in on loving the self was
one area I wasn't previously familiar with. I was still
lacking in some self-confidence in my abilities and had

held myself back for years from doing or saying certain things for fear of what others would say or think of me. So I began to say "I love and approve of myself" a few times a day. After a week of saying this, I started to feel a lot stronger. I began to notice that I ceased caring about what other people thought of me. This was very freeing. I had a nasty rash on my lower legs that I used to scratch quite a bit, often in the middle of the night while still asleep. My skin felt like leather and I regularly drew blood as a result of my long nails clawing at my skin. Incredibly, repeating my loving affirmation caused me to stop scratching and the rash cleared up. After investigating Louise Hay's book again, it became clear that the reason behind this occurrence is because our skin has to do with our individuality and sensitivity. Problems often arise when we let other people get "under our skin." When I knew it was okay for me to be myself, my skin healed. Nowadays any underlying desire to scratch my leg soon dissipates after a few renditions of "I love and approve of myself," as it's very difficult to tear at one's skin and say this at the same time! Now the rash is completely gone and my skin has returned to its natural healthy state.

For the first time ever, I went away on a ski holiday last year. It being my first time to ski and not being sporty by any stretch of the imagination, it was definitely a challenge. It takes guts as well as skill to progress and do well in the art of skiing. As I charged down the ski slope wondering whether or not I was going to land on my bottom again soon, the ideas of affirmations came into my head. As the skis crunched on the soft snow, my body tucked in, ski poles under my arms, moving downhill at what seemed to me a very fast pace, I repeated over and over "I am in control. I am confident. I can do this. All is well." When I finally reached the end of the slope, I was happily still in the standing position, feeling triumphant. Later that day I told my friend about my secret. The following day, she kept repeating, "I am an excellent skier" as she successfully sped down the slopes. Later she reported a great improvement in how she felt as a skier.

A few months ago, I left my "safe" office job to pursue a career in healing. This changeover was made easier using many affirmations to conquer the fear. Affirmations have helped me enormously in setting up my new business. Nowadays, I often open my arms wide and affirm, "I allow prosperity to flow into my life" and "my income is constantly increasing." Very soon after I do this, new clients contact me and new opportunities arrive. Only ten weeks after leaving my office job, my practice became very busy and I now often affirm, "I have an abundance of time and energy for my work!"

I regularly read or listen to Louise Hay, Deepak Chopra and Abraham and feel really inspired, uplifted and filled with a huge sense of purpose. I believe that this elation comes from an inner knowing that the words I'm reading represent the truth. Personal experience and affirmations prove to me time and again that we create our own reality, and that our life can be made more joyous and wonderful if we choose. And so it is.

JOURNEY TO WHOLENESS
Renee Beck, New York

*"God always puts angels in our path
to guide us on our journey. . ."*

In May 1999, I started my healing journey. Little did I know my life would be forever changed. The day after giving birth to my second daughter, I discovered a lump about the size of a golf ball on my neck; after several tests, doctors diagnosed a cyst on my thyroid. I arrived home with my new baby and experienced a wide spectrum of emotions. The doctors' advice: undergo surgery. That, they said, would require a seven-inch incision on my neck, with a 70% chance of hitting my vocal chords. I would need to take hormone medication the rest of my life and breastfeeding my new baby would have to be terminated. This literally sent me to my knees crying on the living room floor, praying for answers to the dilemma.

During this crisis, the phone rang. My friend Kimberly suggested I seek one more opinion about my condition and told me about a man in Ithaca, New York who did Network Chiropractic Care. I made an appointment with him and spent one and a half hours in his office. The only words I remember: "the human body is a miracle. We are designed to heal ourselves: you break a bone, you heal; you get cut, you heal; you pull a muscle, you heal." He wanted to give my body some tools to aid in its healing . . . the best option I had heard! I didn't have a clue what I was getting myself into. I knew nothing about alternative methods.

I saw him three times a week. Five months into my care I started having some pain in my joints, not unprecedented: from age three I had experienced intermittent, reoccurring bouts of rheumatoid arthritis. Now I was overwhelmed by the daunting tasks of healing the cyst and acute pain from arthritis. Remember the old adage that things have to get worse before they get better? Well, that took on a whole new meaning.

My condition worsened so much I couldn't manage anything for the children, our home, or myself. My husband carried me to scheduled appointments and took care of my physical needs. My extended family watched over our children and household. I was faced with having to use a wheelchair. This fueled my desire to heal.

I started seeing an amazing acupuncturist, Ann Greenburg, and began reading every self-help book I could get my hands on, one of which was the *12 Stages of Healing* by Donald Epstein. Faithfully, I read the chapters and did the breathing exercises at the end of each chapter . . . amazed at what began to happen. I started having huge emotional releases and then pain would dissipate for a while. I felt like I was onto something big, so continued to dig into my "pain," and it became evident just how much suppressed emotions were crippling me.

I believe now that we spend years running from our pain because we don't want to face it, or don't know *how* to face it. Finally, the pain screams loud enough to get our attention. Then we suppress it, remove it, or medicate it; very few seek other answers.

I'm so glad I sought for alternative answers. I am thrilled to say I have no cyst and no arthritis present in my body. I am very proud to say: I didn't take any medications or have any surgeries as suggested by my medical advisors.

When you're healing, surround yourself with positive and supportive people. Try doing some form of breath work. Somato Respiratory Integration (SRI) was my choice. Pray, meditate, and pay close attention to the people who just happen to come into your life, because nothing is a coincidence. God always puts angels in our path to guide us on our journey. Special thanks to all my angels!!

In addition, while you're healing be sure to share your experiences with others. That is how we can change our world.

IT'S NEVER TOO LATE

Susan Roberts, England

"Affirmations have been a revelation in taming my inner critic, transforming my thoughts and beliefs as well as keeping me focused on my dreams. . ."

W hen I first came across George Eliot's quote, *"It's never too late to be what you might have been."* I was stopped in my tracks. For some reason, on that rainy day in February it struck a chord and triggered a myriad of thoughts and questions:

What might I have been if I'd been brave enough?

Why am I denying myself the chance to feel truly fulfilled?

Success isn't for people like you – be realistic, be practical.

Dreams are just that – "dreams" – they're not reality.

What am I so afraid of?

What's stopping me?

What if it all went wrong?

What would people think?

George Eliot's eleven simple words allowed me to dare to think it was possible to achieve my ambitions. This quote opened a door I had kept securely locked in order to keep me safe in my 'comfort zone' and to protect my dreams from being tarnished forever by failure. I realised that the term 'comfort zone' is a misnomer when self-esteem is low. However alluring, the reassurance that comes from familiarity and a reduced threat of failure, is a place of denial, endless excuses and frustration. Whatever comfort it professes to offer is offset by the courage and success I deny myself and the denial of realising my dreams. I had allowed 'making a living' and self-limiting beliefs to get in the way of achieving what was most important. Ambitions remained on the "some day" list and "some day" never came. My best intentions were rarely given the chance to become reality.

There wasn't a moment to lose. If it's never too late to be what I might have been, I needed an action plan that would maintain the momentum of this moment. I treated myself to a beautiful journal and ensconced myself in my favourite coffee shop. It was a wonderful feeling being completely absorbed in capturing my thoughts on the receptive and non-judgmental pages of the journal; when I looked up, day had turned to night and the rain into mesmerising snow flakes. A great sense of achievement swept over me as I reviewed my action plan:

ASPIRE
> A—Ambitions
> S—Self-talk and Affirmations
> P—Patience and Persistence
> I—Implementation
> R—Reward and Review
> E—Enjoy and Explore

A for Ambitions:

"I felt as if I were walking with Destiny, and that all my past life had been a preparation for this hour."
–Winston Churchill

As I crunched through the snow back home on that February night, Churchill's eloquent words completely captured the serenity and sense of purpose I felt. It was as if a sudden sense of completeness had enabled me to be in touch with my inner wisdom. *What could be more rewarding than helping others live their best life?* That night I set a goal to be an inspirational and outstanding personal development coach and trainer, and pledged to anchor this fantastic feeling as a motivator to achieve my goal.

Over the next few weeks I wrote my Ideal Working Day including as much detail as I could so whenever I read it, I felt as if I were already there. I also created a Treasure Map Journal using pictures from magazines. This visual representation of my fabulous new life has proved to be a wonderful boost on days when my dream seems far away. Now that some of the ambitions have begun to manifest themselves, both the Ideal Day and the Treasure Map are a great record of my progress.

S for Self-Talk and Affirmations:

A concerned inner critic very quickly interrupted even the compelling sense of pride and fulfillment I felt as I embarked on my coaching studies:

What makes you think you'll qualify?
This is too good to be true.
Who do you think you are?

I describe my inner-critic as concerned because I believe it has good intentions. Like a weakness is often an overdone strength, an inner-critic is an over-protective guardian; in this case not wanting me to fail. Being

100

aware of my self-talk allowed me to identify the underlying self-limiting belief—I am not good enough. Awareness of this belief enabled me to take control of my inner dialogue. When I notice a critical remark or a fear-based question, I simply thank my inner-critic for its concern and change the thought into a more empowering one. Regularly tuning into my inner-dialogue has been really enlightening. I must admit it was rather disturbing at first as it was so derogatory, but slowly and surely the critical words became far more empowering.

Affirmations have been a revelation in taming my inner critic and transforming my thoughts and beliefs, as well as keeping me focused on my dreams. Using affirmations has been essential in the development of my confidence and self-esteem. They have given me the courage to expand my comfort zone, acknowledge my own uniqueness, and become increasingly aware of my self-worth. It's only now as I review my progress in my journal that I realise the synergistic effects that visualisation, positive self-talk and affirmations have had.

P for Patience and Persistence:

"Our greatest glory is not in never falling,but in rising every time we fall." –Confucius

Critical to success are patience and persistence. When you are determined to make big changes in your life it's easy to be impatient with progress and knockbacks can easily be used as an excuse to give up. Years of habitual thinking patterns and limiting beliefs can't be changed overnight; changing beliefs can be compared to adding drops of white paint to a tin of black paint—the colour change will be negligible at first, but in time will change to an ever lighter gray until eventually it will be white. Some of my old beliefs were frustratingly reluctant to be replaced. However in time as the evidence grew in favour of more empowering beliefs, they were forced to admit defeat.

I for Implement:

"What am I going to do today to close the gap between what I am doing and what really matters most to me?" –Hyrum Smith

Below, an excerpt from William H. Murray's book *The Scottish Himalayan Expedition*, says much about the power of implementation:

*"Until one is committed
there is hesitancy,
the chance to draw back,
always ineffectiveness.*

*Concerning all acts of initiative,
there is one elementary truth,
the ignorance of which kills countless ideas and
splendid plans:*

*That the moment one definitely commits oneself,
then Providence moves too.
All sorts of things occur to help one
that would never otherwise have occurred.*

*A whole stream of events
issues from the decision
raising in one's favor all manner
of unforeseen incidents,
meetings and material assistance,
which no man could have dreamt
could have come his way.*

*I have learned a deep respect for one of Goethe's
couplets:*

*Whatever you can do, or dream you can, begin it.
Boldness has genius, power, and magic in it."*

I keep these and other quotes with my affirmations to be read every day. The first focuses my mind on getting things done to move me towards my goal. The second inspires me. When I first copied them onto a card I had no idea of how insightful and powerful those words would prove to be. I can proudly say that providence does move when I have been brave enough to take action. Opportunities I would never have considered have become available.

R for Reward and Review:

"No one keeps his enthusiasm automatically. Enthusiasm must be nourished with new actions, new aspirations, new efforts, new vision." –Papyrus

Reviewing and updating my goal journal on a weekly basis were critical for keeping on track. On weeks when long hours at work prevented me making real progress, just reading my goals and my Ideal Day, flicking through my Treasure Map, reminded me of my destination and refueled enthusiasm.

I found I often focused on what I hadn't achieved rather than how far I'd progressed, so rewards were key for acknowledging small successes on the way. Watching a favourite film, buying myself a bunch of flowers or having a bubble bath with a glass of champagne surrounded by candles were some of the rewards I have given myself for achieving stepping stone goals.

E for Enjoy and Explore:

"There is no high on earth like the high of realizing even one part of one's dream." –Lauren Bacall

One thing I wanted to factor into my action plan was remembering to enjoy the journey as well as the actual achievement of goals. It's very easy to be so focused on the long-term dream that you forget about enjoying the moment. The exhilaration of achievement, however, cannot be exaggerated and provides the springboard for discovering new dreams. Being awarded a distinction for my written course work, coaching my first paying client, and having a book review published proved the accuracy of Lauren Bacall's inspiring words as well as the wisdom of George Eliot that it is never too late to be what you might have been.

CIRCLE OF ANGELS

Susan Dawn Queen, California

*"Then a translucent angel with female features
and huge wings stood before me. . ."*

Angels have a special way of letting us know that they are with us. Sometimes we don't even notice them and other times they surprise and even shock us with their direct and swift intervention.

I've had some pretty tough challenges in my life. As a child, I was filled with confusion and pain from emotional and physical abuse. My mother was mentally ill and both parents were out of control alcoholics. One day shortly after my 14th birthday, my heart dark with pain, I remember feeling instinctively that "beyond life, death must be a better place." That night my mother had one of her typical delusional episodes, in which she accused me of having sex with my father, and repeatedly beat me, throwing me against the walls, shaking me like a rattle, and slapping me in the face. Crying hysterically, I ran outside the house and into the garden, which was my place for healing. I looked up at the clear sky and the stars were sparkling as if to say "hello." I thought to myself, "That's where I want to go, back to the sky, back to heaven." I begged God to please "take me now." I prayed, "I love you God, please take me home to you." I resigned myself that if God would not take me at that moment, I would deliver myself directly to God.

I walked back into the house, hoping my parents were already passed out, which they were. From a drawer in my bedroom, I pulled a straight edge razor blade that I had stolen from my father. It was new and sharp. At the time I thought it was the answer to my prayers. My judgment was clouded with pain. I had no relatives, nowhere to turn, and no one to talk to. I took the razor and walked into the hall bathroom, painted a dull turquoise. I looked in the mirror at my shimmering long blonde hair, my tired red eyes, and once again I thought to myself, "If this is living I want to be dead." Crying, I looked down at the silver razor blade and secured the door. I had learned the fastest way to slit my wrists and die. I felt that to be free again, I had to physically die. As I sat on the cold brown tile floor, I pulled up my sleeve, trying to gather enough emotional strength to insert the blade. The edge of the blade went into my wrist easily. A trickle of dark red blood started to drip from my wrist. I felt afraid and nervous, but I was determined. I kept pulling the sharp blade up my arm. The blood began to stream out and drip onto the floor. My heart felt heavy and dark, but another part of me felt that I was much closer to freedom.

I glanced up at the window where a small radiant white orb appeared. It floated into the room quite gently, and suddenly became larger than the room itself, filling the room with bright heavenly glow. A pink light appeared within the orb; somehow I sensed that the pink light was full of love and understanding. It came towards me and went directly into my heart. Then a translucent angel with female features and huge wings stood before me. She emanated a bright healing light which my being absorbed. Quite abruptly, a non-physical energy shoved me, causing me to drop the razor blade. Then the angel spoke to me with powerful and penetrating words. She told me: "Now is not your time to die, you are meant to live. Your life will be hard, but your challenges will be part of your teaching in the future. Your purpose is to bring healing, teaching, and light to others."

I was then given abilities beyond reason. The angel reached out with her hand and touched my heart, then my hands. I could see a beautiful white light shining from my palms. She told me, "This is your healing light and you will use it to heal, help, and teach others." She also revealed my ability for psychic visions. She told me not to fear, that I would have the strength to get through all of the challenges in my life and that a circle of angels would always walk with me. Even if I could not feel them, they would be there. Then in an instant, she was gone.

This experience transformed my life. I had gone in the bathroom wanting to die, and came out with a new life. Now I always have faith and trust, I always have my angels, and I have been blessed to see many healings and even a few miracles. I now see life and the world as a big school, with lessons each of us has chosen for our own spiritual growth. I have experienced many situations that may appear tragic, but they are my chosen lessons and as I accept them as my karma, I work through them, healing and evolving.

It is far too simple to think that the physical world is all that exists. I like to think of our souls as diamonds, because we are all multi-faceted and multi-dimensional beings. Learning about each facet of our soul is a purpose we are all drawn to, whether we know it or not. When we feel emptiness within our hearts and know that there must be more to life, we are right! This feeling is our soul talking to us, leading towards a spiritual path. If we ask our angels for answers, we will receive them in many different ways. The answers may intuitively guide us to take a class, or come in the form of a dream, or they may come through a stranger at the grocery store. One way or another we always find our answers, because God is always present and so is your circle of angels.

TRUSTING YOUR INTUITION
Dawn Levy-Maeda, Canada

*"With the help of the Universe our new
little home had fallen into my lap. . ."*

I finally made the decision to leave my husband
of six years. It was very frightening (or should
have been), since I would be taking our two
daughters, then two and five. I'd been contemplating my exit for a long time, but the timing hadn't felt
right—I was waiting for a sign. It isn't important now
what the sign was, but it felt essential to take the necessary steps when I felt confident enough to do it:

1. Tell my husband and our families that it
was over.

2. Find a job.

3. Save/make enough money for first and last
month's rent and a moving crew.

4. Find a home for both my girls and me.

5. Find a sitter to care for my daughters in the
evenings.

Telling my husband and our families proved to be easier than expected. I guess they all saw it coming.

A short while after this, my mother, daughters and I were walking in one of my favorite neighborhoods and decided to stop for lunch at a great restaurant on the lake. As we were sitting there, I visualized working there. There was an obstacle, however: what was I to do with the kids? How could I get in enough hours? My soon to be ex-husband was also working; I couldn't leave the kids until he got home.

At this point I decided to trust in the Universe: I approached the manager and explained my situation. He agreed to hire me and work my shift around my schedule! I realized at that instant that the Universe was working with me.

From where I lived, it took approximately an hour to get to work by public transit, but was well worth it—I was able to save enough money for first and last months' rent and pay for movers in less than a month.

In the service industry, many relationships are formed. I met a wonderful couple, who are still friends, and after some life story exchanges, they decided they needed to find me a man. I thought about what they said as I walked away from their table, and suddenly stopped as I intuitively knew to request their help to find a home to rent in the neighborhood rather than find a new man.

Two days later they came back to the café with exactly what I'd requested! I made the necessary phone call and, upon meeting the individual, realized the truth that indeed, *ask and you shall receive.* I had found the ideal home for my little family at a price I could afford, in the neighborhood where I wanted to live! He didn't check my credit and since I had claimed bankruptcy a short time before, this was a very important element. I gave him the first and last months' rent that very day and we moved in two short weeks later. With the help of the Universe our new little home had fallen into my lap!!

My next concern after the move was finding a sitter. I decided to put up a sign on the telephone poles on my street and see what would happen. Within two hours I received two calls; the second was from a young girl who was very flexible and lived only a block and a half away from us. Her parents didn't mind her working late two nights per week and I didn't have to pay her all my earnings. She was my permanent sitter for just over two years—and always there when I needed her!

Everything happened so easily and effortlessly. I know that following my intuition and knowing that the Universe had its way of taking care of things got me where I was supposed to be.

Know that wherever you are right now is exactly where you're supposed to be . . . trust in the powers of the Universe, and know that tomorrow you'll be exactly where you **want** to be.

COMING HOME
Selidia Juniis-Johnson, New York

*"Thus armed with the great wisdom
my parents had imparted,
I set sail on the sea of life. . ."*

Picture a skinny little brown-skinned girl sitting on the steps of her family's Brooklyn brownstone home taking in the passing neighborhood scenes—that was me. People were always talking around me, forgetting I was there, quietly listening and thinking about what they said. Our next-door neighbors from the West Indies always talked of Trinidad, their home. My family was from the South and spoke about "home" too: Virginia. I sat on our front steps and wistfully wondered: *where is my home . . . my real home?* Surely life must have more meaning than what I knew. Someday, someone would come and tell me who I am and where my true home is.

Life revolved around family. I loved to hear the stories about their lives, past, present, and future. Daddy was Superman to me. He had skills, a carpenter who could build anything you could imagine. My Father was also a welder, a cook, a teacher, a deacon, a mason, a leader, a true loving family man; he disciplined with love and fairness. I remember his business card, "If in doubt, call Paul." "Shoot for the stars," he'd say, "Aim high; you may not hit the moon but you'll catch a star." Daddy was strength; I miss him still.

My Mother, 'Mummy', always the peacemaker, was a former hairdresser and schoolteacher. She was a gentle, wise woman, with a kind way who had a saying for everything. I call her sayings, "Mummy-isms." Life has taught me the value of her words: they're the basis of many beautiful truths and words of ageless wisdom.

Most of her *Mummy-isms* came when I was doing ordinary things. Since she was a hairdresser, having my hair done was magical because I had mom all to myself. Every woman knows the bond that happens in that special time when you talk with your hairdresser, both sharing some of your most intimate and profound thoughts and concerns about life. Sitting there with my head back against her, all was well in my world.

Her colorful stories about growing up in the south, the third child in a family of 10 siblings, were plentiful. These stories were like hearing Aesop's Fables because all carried a moral. Grandpa wanted one of his children to teach at the schoolhouse he'd helped to build with the community elders. Mother fulfilled his dream. Life hadn't been easy but she adopted a positive outlook that became her way of handling life experiences. She'd often say, "Take low," but what she meant was to take the high mental road. Also: "don't argue just to win, you may win that battle, but lose the war. Be quick to forgive; do not do tit for tat. Don't speak when you're angry; you never regret what you don't say unless it is I love you, because you can catch more flies with sugar than with salt. You do right for right's sake, not because the other person deserves it. Look for the good in everything and everybody."

When I had household chores, I knew they were subject to inspection and the last thing I wanted to hear about was my attitude in performing the task. I'd get it anyway: "If a task is once begun never leave it 'til it's done, be your task great or small do it well or not at all." Now if I even thought: *well, next time I'll do it not at all,* I'd get this look that could wither a tree, and her famous words, "Now you know better." Even if my chore passed inspection and was pronounced good, she'd deliver the well-known quote: "good better best, never let it rest until your good becomes better and your better becomes your best."

Of course as children we fought with one another and Mom would settle that with the final words: "kiss and make up. After all, pretty is as pretty does, a pretty face may open a door, but a bad attitude will slam it shut." So while I'd be sulking about the real or imagined injustice, she'd say: "Fix your face, girl, and walk like a Maltese kitten, tip, tip, tip in the face of life's adversities." Other sayings I remember: *But if you have to kill your enemy, then kill him with kindness. Turn your hand to help, don't wait to be asked. Remember now the race doesn't always go to the swift but to him who endures to the end.*

Thus armed with the great wisdom my parents had imparted, I set sail on the sea of life. The wind blew and my boat took on some water. Sometimes I paddled with one oar, but *Mummy-isms* always helped me stay on course. Even so, my life was in total disarray. My marriage failed; I had the total responsibility for my beautiful little son. How could I guide him, when I didn't know how to survive this? We'd go to sleep very early—I was trying to get through another night, another day of growing despair.

One night I awakened, having slept what I thought was the entire night. *Oh God it's only 10 P.M.* I turned on the television and "Soul" hosted by Ellis Haslip came on.

He announced, "Tonight we have with us 'The Empress of The Gheez Nation.'" With no explanation my heart leaped and I sat up and took notice as joy filled my soul. The Empress' words had the authority of One Who Knows; the Empress (now passed on) spoke about the pluralistic society in which we live. She defined the word democracy in a way that made sense; she spoke about the need to obey the laws of God. Her words opened up new avenues of thought and a greater understanding. Something within said *yes, this is truth. God is fact, not myth.* Her words found a home in me. The tiny prayer said by a skinny little brown-skinned girl sitting on the steps of my family home had been borne on the air currents and wafted all the way to the highest heaven. The Universe, the Cosmic Kitchen, had responded to my command, sending the answer to my prayers. She taught—no, reminded me, that <u>I AM</u> one with Spirit and Spirit is All there is. Spirit in me, as me, through me, I am a child of the Most High God. My elder brother, The Great Master Jesus The Christ, Is One with the Father Mother God. He walked, talked, and acted in Cosmic Consciousness, an awareness he said I had a divine right to.

What an "Ah, haa!" Learning Divine Science sparked my remembrance. *Mummy-ism's* had been a good foundation for my evolving spirit, and now I had the rest of the picture. Spirit is Source, Spirit is First Cause, Love is Law, Cause and Effect, the Law of Attraction—these immutable laws govern life. My expanding awareness brought me home to my real self. I dwell, live, move and have my being in Spirit, the One Mind. We all dwell in the One Mind. **You too can come home.**

EARTHLY ANGELS

Melissa Ann Privett, Michigan

*"Be careful how you treat people because you
just might be entertaining angels. . ."*

As I sit here in my office-memory room, I
recall scenes from the past: a flower bed
of roses made from Playdough, a Mother's
Day gift from my older son, now 25; a poem written
by my other son when he was 7 that won a contest in
the newspaper 10 years ago. I'm truly a proud mom
and incredibly grateful to be here, for my early years
were filled with so many dysfunctional situations and
obstacles I never thought I'd be able to climb out of
the swamp I was in.

It's easy to agree that one of the most challenging
jobs on this planet is to be a parent. One job far tougher
is to be a single parent without any spousal support. Up
until one year ago, I raised my sons alone. Although my
ex-husband could never find time to visit my children,
he always found time for harassing me. I never thought
I'd get through those years alive. I was alone with very
little family and fewer friends, yet felt comforted with

a blind faith that things would always work out. Funny thing, eventually they did.

Some challenges as a single parent: Salvation Army Christmases, stealing food so my kids could eat, sometimes working three jobs at a time to pay bills, and still finding myself short. Worst of all, in those difficult times I rarely got to see my children. What kind of a price was this to pay for a devoted mother who loved her children? I often wondered why God put me in such a situation.

My ideas about that have changed over the years and I can tell you one reason why: I believe God always takes care of his children and I am one of them. Have you ever heard the saying, "be careful how you treat people because you just might be entertaining angels? "

I recall one grim day many years ago. My oldest and only son at that time was 6. I had lost my job; the utilities were turned off, and I was in the process of being evicted from my apartment. I'd called my brother, who lived about 2 hours away, to ask him if he would please take my son until I could get "back on my feet." Although he was struggling with his own family, he said yes.

In other, similar times, I'd just get up, brush off, and get on with my life. I was tough. I was an island. I didn't need or want anyone's help. I could do it alone. Silly me! Foolish pride found me alone and hungry too often.

I vividly remember that lonely day, sitting in my kitchen by candle light, no electricity, food, or phone, about to be evicted, no friends and no child. The latter hurt the most, and I completely broke down. I never cried, but cried then, and cried hard—sobbing loudly, begging, "Dear God, please help me get through this trial! Please help!"

I held a newspaper opened to the classifieds, while I cried harder and harder, then stopped suddenly, as though I'd released the sadness and fear. *Done!* I was guided to look down. I was looking for a job, but it seemed more, as if God himself was telling me to look. I saw an ad for a cocktail waitress. I had cocktailed before in my life since my divorce and truly didn't want to get back into that type of work, but something kept telling me to call the number.

To my surprise, the owner asked if I could come in right away for an interview. "Yes! I'll be right there." I got in my old beat-up Volkswagen (at least I had a car, although it didn't have reverse, and had to be kick started with the clutch . . . but I had a car.)

At the bar, certainly not the classiest of places, I filled out the application. The manager didn't look at my "credentials;" I really didn't have any. I'd gotten married at 16 and had no education to speak of, but had "good looks." I guess that was enough qualification for this job. I was hired on the spot and asked to start immediately. Elated that I'd eat after my shift, knowing I'd make tips, and tips could buy some food, I put on a uniform and took over my section. The night was long and wild, definitely not my kind of place . . . a lot of drunks, and girls treated disrespectfully. Not me. The men left me alone, and I believe my light, from the legions of angels that surrounded me, was too bright for them to even attempt anything.

Nearing the end of the night a man in his early 40's who seemed drunk sat in my section, and my first thought was to refuse to serve him, but that might end up in some type of confrontation. I just wanted to go home with the money I'd made. However, after getting a closer look, I could tell he was distraught, not drunk. He said he wanted to start a tab. I served him a drink minutes later and began to walk away.

Something made me turn around to discover tears in his eyes. I asked, "Can I help you in any way?" And he began to tell his story.

He'd come here for his son's funeral from another state. He had been an absent father and this was the first time he had seen his son in years. I felt a deep compassion for him, although I didn't respect the separation from his son. I knew all too well how absence from children affects their well-being and sense of self. I listened as he said, "I feel so much guilt and sorrow for making such a big mistake, I only wanted to tell him how much I loved him but it was too late."

I tried to comfort him, and sat with this man who was divinely guided to me on my very first night of work to talk to anyone who would listen. The night was late and he only had two drinks while we sat and talked. I spoke of my trials: "I know how it feels to have parental guilt, knowing I've let my children down, although I don't know what it feels like to be in your shoes. I'm deeply sorry for your situation. I can only offer comfort and support."

I assured him that resurrection always followed crucifixion. It was God's promise. *Where did I get THAT information?* I told him Day would follow Night and he would have a second chance somewhere down the line. I told him his son knew how much he had loved him and he could tell him now if he wanted to. He did. It was as if we prayed together that night without really praying. God's presence was so tremendously felt in that little bar between us. Finally, in the end, both of us with tears in our eyes hugged each other good-bye and he left.

The bar was closing and I was cashing out my tickets for the night. I came upon his credit card charge and almost fell to the floor when I read what he'd written in the "tip" space: $350.00, which brought his bill to $359.00 total! I could pay my phone bill, rent, get the lights turned back on, and best of all get my son back, who at this moment I was missing more than ever.

I never went back to that bar again. I found a day job shortly afterward and things were looking up again. I've found life is filled with ups and downs but Day DOES always follow Night. A new day will always bring new opportunities and God will always find you. No matter where you are, you can't hide. You see, he has earthly angels all over the place. They help him find the lost and brokenhearted.

That night, I was sent an earthly angel. I entertained an angel and he entertained me, because giving IS receiving. I gave to him exactly what he needed—listening with my heart open, and he gave to me exactly what I needed. God works in funny ways. Never think you are alone, no matter the situation.

So here I sit in my computer-memory room, in my nice home with a wonderful new husband and three new stepchildren. I lead a happy joyous life and so do my own children. My oldest just gave me my first grandchild. Life is good and so is God. I remember the tests in my life that brought me to this space and time, thankful for each because without any tests, we have no testimony. Find the gifts in your life! You'll find some piece of God that may have gone unnoticed and, I'm certain, a couple dozen angels or so.

GRACE TIME
Delia Regan, England

*"I absolutely did not want or accept the
inevitability of an operation. . ."*

Here I was again at the Women's Hospital, awaiting a routine scan to check that my right ovary was healthy. It had been eight years earlier and whilst attending my eight-week pregnancy scan, the radiographer had discovered an extensive cyst on my left ovary. I was immediately and unceremoniously whisked in to remove the cyst—and the ovary. I was shaken to the core! Nonchalantly, the top surgeon reassured me (amidst the details of the emergency operation) that I was still pregnant with a high chance of carrying through.

Now, with my eight-year-old son at my side, I cheerfully stepped onto the bed and lifted my sweater to have my latest scan. The radiographer seemed unusually hesitant. The comforting words I expected: "It's a perfectly healthy ovary, Delia" never came.

"I'm sorry," she said. "You have two cysts on your ovary which are too big to be folicular (I was told all women have small cysts that fluctuate between the monthly cycles and disappear). Their size indicates the need for removal. The doctor will explain in detail."

The junior doctor, after checking the scan, proceeded to explain the need for a full hysterectomy. His tone and attitude were akin to a hair stylist advising on the correct shade of dye. Anger screamed within me. I held back tears and protests against the diagnosis and attitude of the doctor. I would not allow my son to see or feel my fear.

The doctor was setting the wheels in motion to arrange the operation (although this time it was not an emergency). My mind was reeling: – HRT (Hormone Replacement Therapy) – loss of womb – 40 something – I felt far too young for this experience. He tried to comfort me with his usual words of wisdom and understanding. "Well, you've no desire for more children so what's the problem?" he commented. Tactfully, I refrained from response, not due to politeness but because I was already jumping ahead mentally.

I asked him for three months grace (I wasn't sure why at the time). He agreed and was still babbling something about inevitability as I walked out with my son to the car. I drove home in a daze, trying in vain to summon up all my holistic knowledge and tools. I didn't sleep that night but lay awake questioning the universe, God, Reiki... whatever. Why had these cysts reappeared? Eight years before was understandable. I was suffering from guilt, fear, disillusionment. I was definitely aware of my negative emotions and thoughts contributing to or causing my past health issues, but I was happy and positive now, so why was this happening?

I soul-searched over the next few weeks, managed to put a different slant on the issue and decided to look at it philosophically and positively. It was the only way I knew. Drawing upon humour, I joked about becoming a 'new woman' and related to glamorous female '50 something's' who graced the women's magazines. Comments about "renewed youth with H.R.T." and "how I met my toy boy" created laughter between my husband and myself. I jovially spoke about becoming a lady of leisure after the operation whilst recuperating and practically welcomed the need for an operation. After all, that was being positive . . . wasn't it?

Then, six weeks into the three months something hit me hard. A big mental shift took placc. I absolutely did not want or accept the inevitability of an operation. I vowed then and there to do everything in my power to avoid this operation, to fight it and return to perfect health.

That night I went to bed with a realization that whatever had created the cysts originally could *uncreate* them. I knew I had the ability and proceeded to utilise every healing tool at my disposal. I affirmed perfect health. As I placed my Reiki (energy healing) hands on the region of my ovary, an image came into my consciousness. It was like watching a large screen and I was in the picture. The gynaecologist who performed my first operation and was so reassuring, Mr. Farqharson, was there surrounded by a beautiful white light. I felt an incredible warm glow as he said, "Delia, you don't need an operation—you are HEALTHY." In the warmth of his voice, I fell into the most peaceful sleep I'd had in weeks.

I awoke 'knowing' that I didn't need the operation. When my husband stated, without prompting, "I don't think you need an operation," I answered without an explanation: "I know I won't." The next few weeks passed easily with a contented 'knowing.'

The day of the appointment finally arrived. "Very strange, there are no cysts here, Delia, they can't possibly have disappeared," said the puzzled radiographer. I smiled smugly and mumbled about positive will and manifestation. Mr. Farqharson checked both scans, smiled broadly and without knowing why, and without the white light, said exactly what I had manifested.

"Delia, there are no signs of any cysts. You're as healthy as any other woman. Go home, rip up your appointment card," he said. And added in the nicest possible way: "I don't want to see you here again."

He never has. That was nearly six years ago and I am 100% convinced that the power of manifestation, positive affirmations, hands-on healing and spiritual guidance were all at work.

I AM NOW HEALTHY AND COMPLETELY HEALED!

BE STILL AND KNOW

Barbara Badolati, Michigan

*"This moment of silence became a time
when I felt surrounded by a comfort that
was not my physical form. . ."*

I kept telling myself "pedal faster" as the burnt orange pick-up truck careened down the hill at 45 miles per hour. I was turning left at an intersection along with traffic, but trailed slightly behind the last car as it completed its turn. The truck driver estimated that he would miss this last car turning, unaware of my approach on bicycle. By the time he saw me it was too late for him to even slow down.

I was hit broadside with absolutely no barrier between the truck grill and me. Besides this immense impact, I could feel the teeth of the right bike pedal piercing through my flesh and gouging out the side of my lower leg. My body flew helplessly 36 feet and I hit the pavement numerous times as my body rolled and bounced uncontrollably. Fortunately, I was wearing my helmet and fortunately, no other traffic was moving through the five-lane intersection at the time.

When my body finally came to a stop, there was silence, a quiet stillness between the trauma and when help arrived. This was only a few moments, but for me, it was as if time stood still. In this silence, something told me to stay conscious, to begin healing my body NOW. Without thinking, I found myself taking deep breaths.

This deep, conscious breathing helped me with the pain much like that of a pregnant woman who uses cleansing breathes during child labor. I could sense the life-giving nutrients from the breath permeating every cell of my body. At the same time, these breaths kept me mentally focused.

This moment of silence became a time when I felt surrounded by a comfort that was not my physical form. On the contrary, my physical form was in shock! However, I was somehow reassured that I was 'ok', that I would be 'ok'.

Then people arrived, seeming like actors who had rehearsed the actions they took. Several people kept me from moving, insisting, "Do not look at your injured leg," (probably a good thing) and caring for me in every way they could. Someone called EMS, and yet another redirected traffic. The paramedics were incredible, providing the support my panicked and injured body needed while rushing me to the nearest hospital. When I arrived at the hospital, my mother and her neighbor gave me endless love and encouragement, and the surgeon did a beautiful job of mending my lower leg with 144 stitches. Besides these human "angels," I believe there were ethereal angels assisting me in this healing process too.

At this time in my life my overall circumstances were quite grim. In fact, one of the reasons I was bicycling was due to not having any other form of transportation. A few months prior to the accident I had been given an option of going to California and beginning a new life there. This opportunity never felt "right" to me, but I had convinced myself that it would be a solution to my current life circumstances. My plane ticket had been purchased and the few possessions packed, ready to fly out the following day.

There have been so many times that I have allowed my thoughts to rule my life— and allowed my mind to "convince" my Self. I've learned to be logical, a common practice in our society. I have learned to make decisions based on weighing the pros and cons rather than from my heart or my intuition. There are times I've prayed and asked for guidance, but then haven't listened. Or if I listened to my intuition, didn't trust and believe it to be what was best for me.

In hindsight, my intuition was speaking to me from the moment the California opportunity presented itself. As I mentioned earlier, I did not have a good "feeling" about going, but logically it looked like a decent alternative to where I was in my life. Perhaps it was my wiser, God-Connected Self that knew this was not the road I should take. Perhaps it was Divine Intervention on that five-lane intersection that FORCED me not to board the plane to California. Perhaps there was no way to get my attention other than to literally knock me off course. And perhaps, ironically, it was no "accident" at all.

It is my belief now that there are no "accidents" or coincidences. It's my belief that the people and events which are in our lives are here to help us become the best that we can be . . . to be on the path that is true for us. I believe that angels, guides and teachers assist us, even in what we perceive to be a traumatic, life-threatening event. But at the time of the accident I didn't believe any of this. I was already "down and out" in so many aspects of my life that I couldn't understand how God could "do this to me."

127

While in the hospital someone had given me the book, *When Bad Things Happen to Good People.* As I began to read, I immediately related to this book. I had played by the rules of life, and it seemed that LIFE had dealt me an unfair hand. However, as in this event, there are some things which we do not understand at the time.

My body was bruised and had turned every color of the rainbow over the next several months. The pain of rehabilitation was excruciating. However, this time of recovery was also a time of discovery. During the physical healing process, I had the time and opportunity to heal both emotionally and spiritually. *I began to listen.* Some refer to this as God's Voice, a Higher Self, an internal guide, or one's intuition. I *listened* through my heart. I *listened* through Mother Nature. I *listened* by being still. Be still, and know I AM God, Psalms 46:10.

Hopefully, you don't have to be put in physical pain or jeopardy for you to listen. Perhaps being aware of the obstacles, which keep you from listening to your God Voice, Higher Self, internal guide, or intuition can help. A wise and wonderful teacher of mine, Rick Nichols, identified these four obstacles as being:

1. Denial – we hear on some level, but we don't want to hear.

2. Lack of Confidence – we don't trust our intuition and hunches so shut them out.

3. Impatience – we are too busy to take the time to look within and listen.

4. Mind – we are locked into facts, methods and tangibles.

I am grateful for that beautiful, sunny spring day and all the people who were there and chose to help me. We all have those "turning points" in our lives, which have shaped us into who we are today. I know this event was one of those turning points for me, and I love who I am today because of it.

Somehow, in some way you will always be guided to your truth, to your path. It may take a day or years, it may be a physical wake up call or a chance meeting. It may be unpleasant, scary or challenging. You may take a detour, a nap or a vacation, but eventually your True Self will put you on your path again. The choice is how soon you wish to listen.

For me, being physically immobilized caused me to lie still and start listening. This put me on my right path again. It was difficult, but that accident was a valuable teacher. It taught me to listen more deeply to myself. To this day, one of the ways I listen closely is through my physical body. Whenever I have persistent physical pain, it's an indication that something is not in harmony within me or within my life. Sometimes I ignore it or take an aspirin. This is that detour, nap or vacation I'd mentioned; eventually, I come around. My body is one of my barometers to being on my true path. Besides all of the millions of ways our bodies serve us, this is yet another. Our body gives us feedback; our job is to listen.

I encourage you to listen. Listen! Listen whether it is through your body, heart or spirit. Above all else, listen and be true to yourself.

GIFTS

Carrie Thomas, South Wales

"I started a healing session on Olivia,
unaware that what was about to
happen would amaze us both. . ."

E ven when bedridden and totally dependent on others because of the exhaustion of Chronic Fatigue Syndrome (CFS or ME), I knew the illness would bring gifts. Not that I accepted being ill; not that every particle of my being didn't fight against the crippling condition; not that I knew if I'd ever totally be well again—but somehow, I always believed the disablement carried its own wisdom and gifts beyond the dreadful daily reality.

One gift was a miraculous step of recovery immediately after writing an affirmation to Christopher Lloyd of Great Dixter, saying that I WOULD once again visit his wonderful garden. From then I was able to spend 5-6 minutes upright at a time, freedom indeed from lying down! Another affirmation at that bedridden time was:

130

My body is healing,
and I will be feeling
so well, and cheering
– on Snowdon*

*the highest mountain here in Wales

When I was told that walking would be the best therapy, I mustered every ounce of energy and walked my 4 minute marathon in a meditative state with the continual affirmation: '*Not only is this GOOD for me, but it's the VERY BEST thing for my body right now*'. And so my gift of 'walking therapy' began: after just nine months I climbed my first mountain, and later indeed *did* cheer wildly on climbing Snowdon! And yes…I've confirmed my first affirmation by visiting the fantastic garden at Great Dixter.

And during those years of illness I developed healing gifts that bring me so much energy and joy! The gift of 'second sight' allows me to see blockages in others' bodies. With heaven's help and the person's permission, I can ease or remove the problem. The gift of 'clairaudience' gives me divine wisdom to channel in order to help people understand and pass through their difficulties with ease and joy. For example, Jeremy had been in a car accident and I saw his head was out of line with his body . . . displaced over the right shoulder. Channelled wisdom explained how the accident 'spoke' to Jeremy about the need to 'realign' his life. When he was able to follow his heart he would be doing the very best things possible. I saw Suzannah as having earplugs in both ears and she agreed there were things happening currently that she 'didn't want to hear'. Divine wisdom was able to offer useful ways of coping, without the issue itself being discussed. In fact, it's usual for me to have no knowledge of what trauma or issue actually created the energy block; it is enough that the individual understands.

It's wonderful to help others discover the gifts inherent in their own lives. But none were clearer to me than Elizabeth. I saw her with a full, strong hip area containing her unresolved past issues as egg-like pebbles. She 'gave birth' to them to expel them from her body, and then I saw them as beautifully gold-wrapped and beribboned Easter eggs. The message was that they were now available for her to inspect, at more of a distance, and to perceive the hidden gifts within the experiences.

This healing gift even works whether I am physically with the person or not, as we can link by phone. June accepted her 'terminal breast cancer' (her words), and was ready to lay her body aside, although wishing she could see her children grow up. I saw a great emptiness where her breast had been, but saw the other breast as an enormous, nurturing area. She explained that she had continued to breastfeed from that side after the mastectomy, and I channelled "there is a balance in all things, as one part becomes disabled, there is a compensating enrichment of another part of the being. It is ever so. It can be no other way—it is merely a part of the laws of spiritual nature that all things are equally balanced at all times." I became aware of her medical consultant as a rather officious, bullying person, and she explained that she'd broken several of his express rules, in particular suffering his wrath when she continued to breastfeed her baby. I saw an image of a can of sardines being opened with its key, and understood: her consultant had been 'opened up' by her disobedience, realising that his rules may not be right. I explained how her defiance already carried a wonderful gift: the specialist now allowed other patients to continue to breastfeed. It was a gift to June to hear how she was already helping other cancer sufferers: effecting change within the institution of the hospital, and changing the specialist's strict views.

Still the gifts come to me: how well I remember the very first body organ I spoke with! For the previous six months, Jill had been doing everything possible to encourage her thyroid to start producing thyroxine again. Her thyroid started talking to her through myself, explaining how it was scared to make more thyroxine, since last time it worked properly, 'it got burned'.* Moreover, 'mummy' was asking it to make something she didn't even like . . . it was very obvious to the thyroid that Jill didn't like thyroxine because she hated taking the replacement tablets. Her thyroid felt under too much pressure, so instead a 'higher' approach was needed: I worked with her pituitary to help the situation. Then I 'felt' her tablets in my hand and was overcome with awe and wonder at the remarkable feats of modern medicine that made taking such a hormone possible. Jill saw my awe with a sense of astonishment: she'd never considered medicine like that (nor had I!), and could now see herself able to take thyroxine with amazement, appreciation and gratitude. *(I was later told that her thyroid was indeed burned, by radiation, to stop its initial overactivity.)

I asked if she knew anyone who had been gifted with life by modern medicine, and the thought of an old friend came to mind. His body had been rebuilt after a car-crash. Without modern surgery he would have died. She text'd him on her mobile: 'Hey, how're u doin?' 'NEVER BEEN BETTER' came his reply. Now she had the affirmation she needed.

I started a healing session on Olivia, unaware that what was about to happen would amaze us both. She said that she had a scar on her side from an old surgical operation that wouldn't heal properly. I saw a spear in her side. How to explain this tactfully? "It's a past life issue," I ventured. "Yes," she agreed, saying she thought she had 'a spear in her side!' "And I've also got a problem here," she said, indicating under her nose. Another difficulty: how to sensitively say that I saw the trouble as a big fat parasitic maggot buried under her skin (again, a past life issue, I felt). Tentatively I said, "I think it's a parasite." Yes," she agreed, "in a dream I saw it bury itself there and go through my body," (here she indicated its route), "and it came out here, on my knee. And there's also something wrong with this foot." This time I saw a dagger struck through the foot, whereas she herself felt another spear. I wondered *who do I know that could help with these issues?* Then I heard within me that I would have the gift to help Olivia to clear it all. I was led to work removing the spear and knife, and healing the resultant 'wounds' with the help of my flower essences. With the parasite, I worked under the nose, then chased though the body using the path traced out by Olivia, until I got to the knee and completed much more clearing there. Doing intuitive healing I never cease to be amazed at some of the things I see and hear, and am led to do, but this has been one of the most interesting, especially when Olivia asked if I wanted to see the scar where the parasite had come out. She rolled up her trouser leg, and there, under the knee was a small circular scar, where, she said, the parasite had come out of her body in the dream!

And as for me, although I always knew the illness of CFS/ME would carry gifts within the disability, I never dreamed how rich, strange and wonderful they could be. These gifts of healing help not only the people I work with, but also help me. Firstly, I'm also listening to those channelled messages and learning from the divine wisdom contained in them. Secondly, it brings me such joy helping others in so many ways, such as removing blockages, and in enabling them to progress more smoothly through life. And finally, I appreciate these gifts because channelling the healing force also charges me with energy, and powers me through my own life and health issues. So thank you, God, for the gift of ME, and the start of a fascinating new life!

ROTTEN WEATHER
Lottie Devontree, Canada

"I experience the wind and rain and
dust because I am alive. . ."

I live in a region of Canada that is considered a desert but for the past week we have experienced the refreshment of rain. The smell is beyond description . . . it refreshes the lungs and cleanses all the cells in my body. Dust settles and grass and plants grow. They are all used to soaking whatever moisture is deep within the earth or mechanically offered with our sprinklers; now it seems as though they are reaching high into the sky with a relaxed joy.

I feel this joy as well, and appreciation and gratitude is abundant . . . so wonderful to live in a climate where the weather changes constantly, sometimes a few times a day.

I'm reminded of my teacher who speaks of the experience of weather as a choice. Someone can look outside and see the dust that our severe winds produce and say, "What a horrible day—such rotten weather." That is their experience. Or I can feel the power of the wind against my face and see how people struggle to walk, how large trucks wait at the side of the highway until the wind subsides. The drivers know their entire unit could be catapulted into the ditch on its side if the wind isn't given respect, a powerful reminder of how little control we humans really have. When I accept that, I can embrace the weather and marvel at it and say, "What an amazing day. I feel so lucky to experience this." That is just as true for me as someone who finds this day a wretched one.

It brings momentary sadness when I hear the complaints about the inconvenience of weather. I experience the wind and rain and dust because I am alive. I can feel it. It is just there, and not controlled by my wishes or schedule of events.

I'm laughing now at the ignorance, the not knowing I could have enjoyed this many years ago—I simply didn't know or feel lucky to be alive. I thought I needed to accomplish things, to gain some status and recognition. There may be a time for bemoaning and grieving the time that was lost, the not knowing, the scrambling in all sorts of frantic and harmful ways to feel that feeling of aliveness again. What is so absurd is that when too much time is spent in the rehearsal of what was lost, more time is lost.

Now time for me represents a breath, the preciousness of each breath. Life rides on each breath and gives me one more moment to experience joy. Not the kind of joy that is dependent on weather or anything I might not like in my external world. Today, I can feel a feeling inside of me that has no words. I can call it Truth or God or Peace or Joy and those words are all less than the reality of my experience. That feeling liberates me daily from the ignorance and illusions that my mind creates. Each day I pray for the courage to accept this magic in my life. My gratitude is so immense for the discovery of that place.

I suspect that being a human being is about feeling that deep joy and enjoying as much as is possible in our everydayness and then shedding most of the garbage we have experienced from others and getting on with the business of enjoying again.

How long does it take to shed the garbage? That is the piece I don't understand. As long as it takes, I guess. Why not sooner? Why can't we get *it* sooner? I don't know. We don't get it until we get it. That requires an abundance of acceptance and acceptance is about feeling. It seems to be a release of the question of why and an integration of this moment called Now; a deep yes, over and over again. Great courage is required, great, great courage.

It is time to laugh. Ha! Ha on me! The weather does what it does and I can simply experience it and enjoy. It is that simple.

ARE YOU YOUR OWN WORST ENEMY?

Beverly Staley, California

*"Our beliefs can either cripple and keep us stuck
in life, or lead to positive goals and dreams. . ."*

How many times has the phrase "You're your own worst enemy" been directed at you? I've have heard it many times in the past and promptly dismissed it as a cliché, not taking it to heart and certainly not exploring it more deeply. Over time, as I've had more life experience, education and training, I see clearly the truth that we often are our own worst enemy.

At a young age, as our socialization begins, our inner critic is born, initially to help us set standards and to protect us. We have parents, teachers and others who begin to shape our self-image, perceptions and internal dialog. Some of the harsh criticisms and perceptions we had as children are kept alive in present time through the voice of the inner critic. I believe, as do many who have written about this, that the inner critic is a sub-personality and is always with us.

In my adult life, for many years I kept alive what I considered a "difficult" past. From my earliest memory at about four years old until age nineteen, I lived with my family in a series of homes that were ugly, old, and non-traditional for living quarters. Though my mother kept our living space spotless and always cooked good meals for us, and my father worked hard to provide the true necessities of life, the structures that housed us were not houses. We lived in large brick buildings, a converted library building on a church property, the back of restaurants and house trailers. I had terrible judgments about this and, I now realize, projected this onto others and felt the shame of 'their' judgments. At nineteen I moved to California from the Midwest where I grew up, but I didn't move away from the feelings.

Because of the vulnerability, I felt I was always working hard to look good enough personally, to live in a beautiful-enough environment, to be nice enough, have my children look good enough, etc. This created tremendous anxiety that ultimately resulted in panic attacks and a breakdown in my mid-thirties with undiagnosed agoraphobia (an abnormal fear of being in crowds, public places and open areas).

I began to read voraciously and desperately to help myself, and was fortunate to discover a book, *Hope and Help for Your Nerves* by Dr. Claire Weekes that launched my recovery process. I practiced a formula presented in her book and was gradually able to get back into the outside world. I began my college education, still with anxiety, but with confidence that I could handle extreme anxiety or panic. I studied psychology, earning a Bachelor's Degree and went on to get a Master's Degree in Marriage, Family and Child Counseling.

My deeper healing journey began with my discovery of *The Power of Your Other Hand* by Lucia Capacchione, Ph.D. About the same time, in 1989, a close friend and colleague introduced me to another of Lucia's books, *The Creative Journal.* She and I began attending weekend retreats with Lucia, applying her methods of expressive arts, creative journaling and the Visioning® process to our own lives and the lives of our clients. I learned through this work that I had irrational beliefs and a critical inner voice that were limiting me and contributing to my anxiety. In 1999 I completed a year long intensive study with Lucia and became a certified instructor and supervisor for her and mentor to many of her students.

As a part of my graduate school training I joined a psychotherapy group of women therapists. With this support and the self-awareness I was gaining from the expressive arts processes, I began to nurture and value myself, dream big, believe my dreams would come true, challenge my critic, and get more balance in my life. Along with my private practice I began giving workshops introducing others to these life-enhancing methods.

With the journaling, psychotherapy group, and education in the field of psychology and relationship, I began to understand how much my negative self- talk and irrational beliefs were operating in my life—the beliefs and judgments had been deeply buried and didn't seem to have words. I now had a method to help me pay attention to what I actually was telling myself, to separate and sort out my irrational thoughts, to look for objective evidence that the thought was true (it seldom is), and to choose my higher power as a life-affirming resource rather than the automatic critic voice. As I look back, I remember only that I felt anxious and had some undefined, non-specific sense that I was flawed, not good enough, somehow didn't measure up to others and this was related to not having the foundation of a "normal" childhood home.

I can clearly see now, as I have worked with all this, that I kept the anxiety alive by the negative self-talk instigated and exaggerated by the unconscious irrational material. After all, it's irrational to believe that I was in any way less of a person merely because what gave me shelter as a young person looked different or ugly to me. These underlying beliefs lived within me, notwithstanding that I had a good deal of confidence in my skills and abilities in many areas, had created a very nice life with my wonderful husband and children, had a beautiful home, and accomplished many things. The problem was that the accomplishments were limited (compared to what I now see as my potential) and accompanied by much unnecessary and ultimately crippling anxiety.

I heard a life coach remark recently that it is not with a person's perfection that we connect, but rather their imperfection. Yet we often strive for perfection and attempt to hide our flaws. Interesting, isn't it?

The work of extricating oneself from the bonds of destructive negativity is a process. There are many books and tools available. Lucia's book, *Recovery of Your Inner Child* is another excellent resource for deep healing.

Hal and Sidra Stone, creators of the Voice Dialog process have written extensively about inner critic attacks. They also write about the positive nature of the critic as an "alarm system, alerting us to the possibility of pain, shame or abandonment." They tell the reader how, in *Embracing Your Inner Critic*, to arrive at "an understanding of the underlying anxiety and fear that motivates" a critic attack "...we ally ourselves with its underlying concerns rather than listen to its superficial complaints" and "find that as we learn to take care of the Critic we are also learning to care for the Inner Child."

It has been my pleasure in more recent years through coaching workshops and private sessions to introduce others to creative journaling and various ways to look at how our beliefs can either cripple and keep us stuck in life, or lead to positive goals and dreams. I believe it is my purpose to share my story and the tools I've learned to help others create their best life, a life that includes joy, peace and passion.

A PATHWAY OF CLUES

Georgina Rodríguez Paz, Mexico

*"Each of us creates a more enlightened
world just by being our true self . . ."*

One night when I was five years old, I dreamt about being with Jesus. Both of us wore clothes like white large tunics and dark clouds were around us. Jesus was standing with a candle in His hand in front of me; there was complete silence between us. My family considered this a blessing, not just a beautiful dream. Once in a while I remember that dream, one of the few I still can remember from my childhood.

Many years later, big changes came to my life, giving new meaning to that image. I was ready to change, tired of not feeling happy about being myself. My first son, Angel, was born a year before, so I wanted to change in order to have a happier life for all of us. I couldn't imagine what changes I could make in thinking, living life, and loving my inner self and my world.

August 8th, 2000: I was working at my office and ran into a co-worker who is now a great friend, Lili Escamilla.

We didn't see each other frequently, but that day began to talk, and she told me about a wonderful book. I already knew a lot of good life improvement books, but she showed me Louise Hay's book: *You Can Heal Your Life* (YCHYL). I'd seen it before and never bought it, but she told me after reading the book her life began to change for the better. Lili was doing the affirmations and what she needed to know came into her life at the perfect time.

I was skeptical. It sounded too easy to believe that just because you affirm something, you make it come true. She asked me not to buy the book because she was going to give it to me as a gift.

So I began to affirm that all I need to know comes to me in a perfect way and time. That same day, I was surprised to see the book in my parents' living room. Mom told me, "That's your sister's book."

Lore told me she bought it because she'd dreamed about it a night before. My mind said: *Surprise, Gina! Your affirmations are working just like life clues.*

August 20th, 2000, I found the book at my desk with a note from Lili: *This gift is not because of a promise but a pleasure to share.* It was amazing. I read that my life begins to change when I love myself the way I am. Louise Hay's words were so tender, so enlightening, that my heart opened to all the new information. I was reading, reading and reading. I bought several CDs and books by Louise and gave several copies of the book to family and friends. While I was healing my life and changing, I saw an advertisement for the Heal Your Life (HYL) workshop. A night before the workshop started, I had a dream which had several doors to choose from. Then I understood it was like one of the workshop exercises ("Doors to close and doors to open"). Another clue!! It seemed that I was in synchrony with my new pathway. Lore and I went to the workshop and it was wonderful.

I had a very old resentment I was carrying and forgave the person and the situation. I also forgave myself for many things. I cried for several days, while feeling "I am in my process of healing." With every moment, I was feeling more love and began to realize all the miraculous things in my life and gave thanks because I was able to notice all these little (and big) day-to-day blessings. I felt whole and complete. My relationships did improve as I was looking for more changes.

I discovered Marianne Williamson's beautiful book, *A Return to Love,* and also found *A Course in Miracles* and many more. Every change became a new clue that led me to the next step. Every year, I went to the HYL workshop in order to continue my "cleaning process." In 2003, after the birth of my second baby boy, Pablo, I came to realize I really wanted to become a HYL Teacher. Searching on the internet, I found a website for a workshop to become a certified teacher. I thought: *Someday I'd like to go to the certification workshop.* So I kept the information and thought about it now and then.

Exactly five years after my first encounter with the YCHYL book, I was on vacation with my husband and our two kids. Meanwhile, Mara Ontiveros, a friend of mine in Mexico City was e-mailing Patricia Crane in order to learn about the certification process to become a HYL teacher. At the beach that day, August 20th, 2005, I found a shell shaped like an angel wing. It was a beautiful coincidence.

On Monday, Mara told me about the next certification workshop: September in San Diego and May in Florida. Certification as HYL teachers was a goal for both of us. I was very excited about the possibility, but had to consider costs of the workshop, hotel, plane, meals, time away from my family, and flying to a foreign country, so close but still other country, culture and language. I was affirming for a clue to show me if I should attend the HYL Workshop in San Diego.

When I went to pick my kids up from school one of the teachers asked me to wait in order to give me my 5 year-old-son's books. Then I saw the clue I'd been waiting for: a science book with a wonderful butterfly of green and purple colors that reminded me of the one which appears on the cover of one of Louise Hay's CDs. At that moment I understood, I _have_ to be at the Workshop. After I talked to my family, asked for vacation at work, got the money for the first payment, and booked the flight, Mara said: "I just realized this isn't the right moment for me to go to the workshop." What?

I wasn't sure if I wanted to go on my own. I felt afraid, but the clues were so clear they left no room for doubts. On September 9th, I was on a plane again, thinking "I just can't believe this," and arrived in San Diego feeling nervous about being alone and not sure if my English was in "good shape" after several years without practicing speaking it.

At the workshop meeting room there was a beautiful group of 10 people from the USA, Greece, England and another girl from Mexico. The teacher training was a wonderful and precious time of healing and learning. I began to feel comfortable with my way of speaking English. My Greek friend Georgette had told me, "Gina, don't worry about your English. You're speaking from the heart."

There were more clues to follow the others! During the training we went to Patricia and Rick's ranch. While doing a meditation exercise, I remembered my childhood dream. Suddenly without even thinking, the image changed and I saw Jesus again . . . this time giving me the candlelight and showing me with that light I could give more light to the world. I understood then that each of us creates a more enlightened world just by being our true self.

After a powerful breathing exercise was over I opened my eyes, and another clue appeared. On the wall was a lovely drawing of a woman emerging from a butterfly I hadn't noticed before. Later that day we did an exercise of walking in a real labyrinth. I was open to receive and understand whatever clues were meant for me.

During that walk I looked down and saw a small black stone with an angel painted on it. I was about to pick it up and take it with me, then realized it wasn't mine to take, but belonged in the labyrinth even though I considered it another clue (clues of butterflies and angels). When I shared all these insights with the group, Rick said the small stone had somehow just appeared in the labyrinth—someone in a previous group must have left it—and he said, "Gina, take the stone because it may have been put there for you, it's not the labyrinth's."

I was so happy I began to cry, knowing now that it was OK to follow my heart in this adventure. Then Patricia said: "Gina, did you say one of your first clues was a green and purple butterfly?"

"Yes," I answered. She replied "Well, I have a tattoo of a green and purple butterfly!" No doubt this was a big clue for me, and maybe for Patricia, too. Who knows?

On my flight home to Mexico, there was a girl with a green and purple butterfly tattoo more visible than Patricia's. I smiled and opened the flight complimentary magazine. The very first page I saw was an article called *The Minotaur's Labyrinth*. So many clues for just a month!

I'm so happy to have followed this pathway of clues and now am one of the seven certified HYL teachers in Mexico. With this great opportunity in my life I want to keep in mind what Georgette had said, "Speak about this training, no matter what language, but always from the heart."

THE SERENITY OF EMBRACING CHANGE

Lynn Koll, Minnesota

"When I take time to breathe and stay in the present moment, my Sage Self gathers its wisdom. . ."

Change and transformation are always in process to evolve us. How we respond to change determines how we evolve. The Serenity Prayer is one of my favorite wisdom prayers about change. It reveals timeless wisdom that has transformed my beliefs and outlook in life. The prayer is magnetized to my refrigerator door, and I am reminded each day of its words:

> *God, Grant me the Serenity*
> *to accept the things I cannot change,*
> *Courage to change the things I can,*
> *and the Wisdom to know the difference.*

Learning to "accept the things I cannot change" is an insight I need to continuously practice. We do not always have the ability to control economic trends, political viewpoints, consumer preferences, technological advances, war, and catastrophic changes in our earth.

148

The best approach to handle these things we cannot change is to accept them. We cannot always choose what happens in our life or society, but we can choose how or if to respond at all.

We live in a world of ever increasing changes and diversity, and it brings me much serenity when I accept that others have and are entitled to their own beliefs, philosophies, and perceived solutions to problems. It is not my responsibility to control or change their minds. My only responsibility is to be authentic and true to myself in how I choose to live, worship, speak and behave. As I honor and validate myself, my self-esteem grows. I stop judging others and seeking approval for my actions. I realize that all people are on personal journeys through life doing the best they can with the level of personal and spiritual growth they have and need at any given moment.

The Serenity Prayer reminds me to have "courage to change the things I can." While I cannot control the occurrence of certain events happening in the world, I do have the power to shift my attitude and find the growth opportunity in each event. With enough courage, I also have the power to change certain circumstances and environments in which I live, work, and play.

It's easy to cling to what is safe, secure and familiar. It takes courage to release fears, speak our truth and follow our hearts. I am inspired by the quote from Chelle Thompson, Editor of *Inspiration Line* , an online magazine, who said "Change has long been a fearful thing for human beings ... and at the same time, it is our most Divine opportunity. Clinging to the banks of the river may seem safe and more secure, but life's possibilities are truly engaged only when we trust, release and become part of The Flow of the Universe."

After 25 years in the business and finance field, I was feeling drained of energy and passion for my job. I felt inner nudges and a tap on my shoulder to follow other life passions. Eventually the taps turned into major blows. I worked through several fears and limiting beliefs about my security and ability to be successful in work I loved. I set the intention that opportunities would come my way to use my gifts and joyfully fulfill my life's passions. I held the feeling, affirmed it, and surrendered to "The Flow of the Universe."

My trust paid off. Starting with the day I turned in my notice at work, I began attracting opportunities to serve in areas I'm passionate about. I was invited to write a contribution for this book, was awarded a PTA grant to teach an awareness curriculum to children at my son's school, asked to give a presentation at a Mom's Club, and invited to lead and co-create workshops and retreats. I thanked the Universe for granting me the "courage to change the things I can" by following my heart and it rewarded me with perfect synchronicities and opportunities to catalyze and energize my life.

The final and most important line of the Serenity Prayer calls for "the wisdom to know the difference" between what to accept and what to change. It takes wisdom to discern when someone wants advice or just wants a listening ear. It takes wisdom to turn discontent into positive action. It takes wisdom to realize that we are all on a journey to learn and discover and that we are responsible for our own choices, attitude and outlook.

The wisdom of the Serenity Prayer reminds me that our individual and collective lives on Earth are constantly evolving. During the time spent reading this chapter, you have evolved. The neurons in your brain have made synaptic connections to other neurons. We are constantly learning and opening our minds to new ideas. Time appears to be speeding up, and unprecedented shifts are happening at all levels.

It feels to me like we are in the middle of highly accelerated times of personal, emotional and spiritual growth. Many ancient philosophers have prophesied these evolutionary shifts. The urgent message from the Hopi elders is, "There is a river flowing right now very fast. It is so great and swift, that there are those who will be afraid. They will try to hold on to the shore, they will feel they are being torn apart and will suffer greatly. Know that the river has its destination. The elders say we must let go of the shore, push off in to the middle of the river, keep our eyes open and our heads above the water… We are the ones we have been waiting for." This affirms to me that all the economic turbulence, warfare, fraud, and earth changes, are expressions of our consciousness and like a river, have their destination and purpose. They are coming to the surface to be revealed, healed and learned from.

In order to rebuild with new visions and intentions, we must banish our fears and embrace change with serenity. The changes in our global or individual evolution cause us to either fight and "hold onto the shore", or take flight and "let go of the shore" toward new possibilities. While change often brings the appearance of chaos and tragedy, acceptance and willingness to change are critical for our own happiness and for humanity's evolution and survival.

Individually and collectively, we do not recognize that we have an innate survival instinct. Until enough tragedy and chaos occurs, many of us don't feel compelled to initiate changes in how we live or view the old, outdated ways of solving problems. If we step "out of the box" and continually create new sustainable ways of thinking, living, and being, positive change will happen. The scarcity of oil may call us to simplify our lives, conserve our resources, utilize alternative energy, and collaborate in our communities. Have you noticed the evolutionary changes in the children of today? For the sake of humanity's future, it would be good to listen to the wisdom that the children have to share; they are here to help us evolve.

Controversy surrounds most every belief held within our political, medical, religious, and education systems. Many give their power away to leaders whom they assume know better than themselves. Most of humanity seems to be living in a trance and must be un-hypnotized from collective subconscious fears and limiting beliefs that keep us small and afraid to make changes. The chaos of change may actually be the necessary catalyst to re-build our institutions based on truth, integrity, equality, sustainability and empowerment for the greatest good of all.

My evolutionary journey of self-discovery over the past several years has helped me become more aware and awakened to remember who I am, was, and want to be. I am practicing each day to honor my journey, release my fears, build enriching relationships, and accept my own imperfections. When I take time to breathe and stay in the present moment, my Sage Self gathers its wisdom and listens to the whispers of my intuition. I realize that my life is just one synchronistic thread on the web connecting all people and nature. When I fill my heart with unconditional love, acceptance and compassion for all people and situations, I reap the benefits that the Serenity Prayer has to offer.

As our lives continue to change and evolve, it becomes increasingly important to affirm our goals and set intentions. Ask yourself questions that open new possibilities, and watch how unseen forces help create the life of your dreams. What could you do to achieve peak energy and aliveness? What fears must you heal in order to "let go of the shore" and live your authentic life? What advice does your inner Sage Self whisper that brings you more serenity, courage and wisdom? Are you ready to let your heart soar? The future may not allow us to sit on the fence any longer. My hope is that we can all see change as a welcome tap on our shoulder and allow it to become our greatest ally to learn, grow, live joyfully and realize our life's greatest mission on Earth.

FROM BUST TO BOOM

Sarah Waters, England

*"The first thing that happened was
a miracle in it's own right. . ."*

It was just another challenging day in my small print business, which I ran with my partner. We had been having a tough time financially and accrued a few debts, but were just about making ends meet when the local court bailiff came through the door. I didn't think too much of it. We had gotten to know him quite well, and he was just doing a job like the rest of us. I signed for his letter, exchanged pleasantries with him and he left. I put the envelope on the side to deal with a customer, and when it all was quiet I opened it.

I still recall with absolute clarity the gut-wrenching feeling as I read the first word:

BANKRUPTCY

This was not what I had expected. I felt like I was on one of those rides at the fair, where they strap you into a big cylinder and then when you're spinning really fast the floor drops away from under your feet.

I was completely horrified at the thought of losing my business, my flat, my whole world. One of our creditors had decided not to wait for his money, so had petitioned for bankruptcy and because it was not a limited company, it was against the business owners.

I knew plenty of other business people who had taken bankruptcy as a way of getting out from under a heavy debt burden, but that was not the way I was brought up. For me the thought of bankruptcy meant I had no integrity or honour and I wasn't prepared to give in and accept what looked like my fate.

I had been working with *You Can Heal Your Life*, somewhat half-heartedly. I knew about affirmations and visualisations, and meditated a bit. But here I was facing a total disaster; this was no time for half anything as I only had a month to get the money together, so I got the book out and started re-reading the relevant chapters.

After a bit of writing and editing I came up with a set of affirmations:

> I can pay all my bills.
> I have enough money.
> I have a thriving business with good
> customers who always pay their bills.
> All the money I need flows into me.

Sometimes I'd just lie there and mumble these affirmations over and over. I'm sure if anyone had seen me they would have taken me straight to a psychiatric ward!

They became a mantra, as much out of total desperation as anything else, but I kept repeating them over and over. At the same time, I spoke to Citizens Advice to find out my rights, I talked to people who had been through the process to glean any bits of useful information, and each evening I sat quietly and visualised handing over a cheque for the full amount to the court bailiff. A friend of mine always says "when you are all at sea, pray to God, but row like heck for the shore." I was definitely doing all the rowing I could.

The first thing that happened was a miracle in its own right: just five days after receiving the bankruptcy petition a cheque arrived for an invoice that we had been chasing for months and had mentally written off as a bad debt. The bill was paid in full with interest.

Then, there was a surge of new customers booking advertising and paying up front rather than after publication. Orders started to increase, and they were always the ones that gave a good profit. Slowly, day by day, the money started coming in. Each day I was walking round the office chanting my affirmations and each night I visualised handing over the cheque.

A couple more old invoices were paid up, and I spent more time on the phone trying to get as much money in as I could. Things had really improved, but with such a tight schedule I was really struggling. The weekend before the hearing, I was still £1500 short of the full amount, and in spite of the affirmations and visualisations I couldn't see how I could make up the extra money.

I went off to visit my parents, but hadn't previously mentioned what was happening in my life. My parents had a good standard of living, but they were not rich, and had never been the sort to have cash sitting about that wasn't needed to fix or replace something. I was by now fairly stressed, which showed very clearly on my face, so I told my parents what had happened and where I was and that it was probable I would be declared bankrupt the following week.

They listened and sympathised and asked questions, and then my Dad said, "I have just had an unexpected tax rebate of £1500; you can borrow it if it helps". *If it helps!* I thought: *It solves everything!* So with such gratitude that has never been seen before or since, I left with a cheque for £1500 in my pocket and the next week I gave a cheque for the full amount to the court bailiff. The account was settled without further costs and the petition was dismissed!

From that day on I have never doubted the power of affirmations and visualisations. I paid my parents back within the year, my business went from strength to strength, and although I have sold out my half, it still thrives today.

I moved onto to new and different jobs, different relationships, all the time knowing that I would always be looked after and always have enough money. Over the years I've gotten even better at aligning with my affirmations. I have studied 'Abraham Hicks' and now know about the "art of allowing," and this makes things even easier. In just over 8 years I have welcomed in a substantial property portfolio, and excellent annual earnings.

I use these techniques in every area of my life, and am blessed in many ways. This is not rocket science . . . it is available for anyone to use, just trust it!

PLAYING IN THE GAME
ON THE FIELD

Corene Walker, New Zealand

*"It was time to re-enact the proverbial
toddler learning to walk: get up, fall down,
get back up again and experience each
portion of this journey as a gift. . ."*

"Once upon a time there was a young child born as a magnificent, flawless diamond and as she grew her beauty shone and her innocence sparkled. From her early teenage years she dreamed of meeting the man in her life, of getting married early, once and forever, having children and living in a beautiful home."

Naturally I progressed from a young teenager to learn there was more to this game of life than a fairy tale story. It became glaringly apparent I needed to learn many different facets of the game called 'Relationships' . . . there always seemed to be new rules. In order to stay on top of the game and its countless rules, I pressed my intelligent mind to exhaustion, and pushed my body and adrenal glands with constant performances trying hard to keep up, to prove I really *was* good enough, and I really *was* lovable and acceptable at home, in school,

158

with my family and friends. However, no matter how relentless my pursuit, my diamond gradually became clouded and the need to prove myself dominated.

Whenever 'the-way-things-were' seemed to offer no possibility; whenever I became confused; whenever I was taken by surprise with my eyes wide open; whenever others refused to cooperate or compromise, or be even half-way decent, then I knew fresh rules were definitely needed.

I thought Playing by the Rules meant being 'nice' and saying all the 'right' things, or a bright happy smile even when tired and I didn't feel like it. I thought it meant trying even harder. It certainly meant losing me piece by piece and giving away my power, although I didn't know it at the time. And I thought it meant prostituting my precious soul for others to walk over, abuse, and manipulate just so I could daily remind myself I was a good person and hadn't done anything wrong, because I was Playing by the Rules.

As I walked through my 20's and 30's, I'd already learned that certain things are lost forever and no matter how much I tried to engineer them, fairy tales can go horribly wrong. But the soul deep inside is never lost. When the soul is ready for the journey of its life and wants to reclaim and reassert itself, the only step is onto the playing field to play the best game of life possible.

At this point, while searching for the missing 'X' factor in my life, I made a radical decision to take responsibility of a different kind—to rediscover I did have "the ability to respond". To have this new responsability, I needed to risk being who I really was. I began shedding the protective layers which had become my shield, obscuring the true innocence and beauty of my inner diamond. It was time to re-enact the proverbial toddler learning to walk: get up, fall down, get back up again; time to experience each portion of this journey as a gift, something to really grin about as the real me was presented to the world.

It was certainly time to respond in a different way to everything that had happened—the mistakes and accidents, each short and long-term relationship that ended abruptly, and the wins and losses of stepping outside the social norm with my careers. Absolutely no one could choose for me: this was my body, my life, and my own choices. Moving on was essential and not as a spectator on the side. I was going to practice being a 'player on the field' making a difference.

Finally, the man of my dreams—mind mapping really works! But be careful what you ask for, because you get exactly that, and the one vital ingredient left off my list of attributes for this ideal partner was health. My real-life ideal man was dying. Coming from a background of rescuers, it was so easy for me to slip back into the old game rules and old patterns. I went back trying to 'rescue', collapsing all my boundaries in order to save this man so we could have a long and happy life together. Even though I was getting really clear, I still had some wounded parts crying out for healing. My ingrained beliefs insisted on holding fast! Definitely not what I wanted for my future.

I realised this pattern had been rampant in every relationship. The buck stops with me, and this was a magic opportunity to finally break the cycle. I would unconsciously give my power away to others, and when I didn't get my way I would 'nicely' manipulate, or get angry and become the victim. It was hard for me to 'get' that what I wanted wasn't necessarily what the other wanted. Especially in intimate relationships, I'd become disappointed and angry because I thought that he should care as much as I did, and then I would try even harder to please. I've since come to realise that people will do what they want to do, and I must respect their decisions. Now when I require respect, I outline my boundaries and ensure that I uphold them even if others don't, by following through on the consequences already set.

Relationships with my family, colleagues, and friends are always so important and their success depends on the way I play the game as a player on the field. To be able to stand in my power with no excuses; to accept full responsibility for my own thoughts, words and actions; to be constantly aware I have the ability to choose my response in any moment; and to experience the pure power that always results from this way of playing is just awesome.

Conversely, if I play the game as a spectator on the sideline complete with criticism, judgement, excuses, reasons, blame and justification; reactively thinking someone outside of me has caused the problem; or simply manipulating openly or covertly to get my way, I always wind up the victim. I've come to be aware that when I'm a spectator my confidence is low and I don't like myself. I inevitably revert to pulling down the energy of others even though this energy gain is only temporary and the relationship is left damaged.

I see that playing on the field is an enormous privilege and has certain risks. Some may choose to stay with me and others may choose to leave. I've realised that someone who stands up to me and is unwilling to accept my rescuing, below-the-line and abusive behaviour is more of an ally than someone who goes along with it, either out of fear or resignation. The stumbling blocks that stand in my way are part of me and only I can remove them. As a result of this breakthrough, I am so much happier with my life and above all I deeply love myself. My real life story is now closer to a good fairy tale and my diamond is given the opportunity to beautifully radiate every day.

When bad things happen I still experience a spectrum of responses that includes guilt, blame, regret, helplessness or resignation, the sense of injustice, righteousness, and anger. Each of these responses actually takes me on a detour away from the real living field and back into the spectator stands. Still at any moment I have a choice to get back on that field.

When I am 'playing on the field' I present no obstacles to others. It's awesome to observe how profoundly dependable I am to the people who work with me, especially if they feel no problem could arise between us that I'm not prepared to own. Imagine the ripple effect if they followed my lead!

While it calls for courage and compassion, this practice launches you and me on a soaring journey of transformation and development. Let's just say that somewhere along the journey we rescued too much, or slipped too often, or heard too many monkey voices in our head and wandered off the track.

What a difference to choose to rescue only myself; to operate within healthy boundaries; and to open to a whole, loving tenderness inside. Rather than commenting from the sidelines, I look around at this day, these people, you and me, and how we all shine brilliantly, exactly as we are in action on that playing field!

WHEREVER YOU GO
THERE YOU ARE!
Rita Martinez, Arizona

*"I began doing yoga and meditating
after hitting bottom at work. . ."*

Recently I moved from New Mexico to Arizona in hopes of escaping my sorrows after my mother's death a few years ago. Prior to my move I witnessed the gradual deterioration of a tight extended Latino family. I realized that mamacita had played a central role in the maintenance of the tight bonds among all my adult siblings. Yes, we had our differences yet frequently got together as a familia to celebrate birthdays, baptisms, first holy communions, weddings, Christmas, Easter and countless other celebrations. There was a lot of togetherness, which at the time I thought was a little much. We seemed to always be at my mom's place for something. As they say, "You don't know how good you've got it until you lose it."

After my mom went on to her next life, I missed her immensely and my relationship with her changed dramatically after I was in Arizona. Following a renewal of faith, which was prompted by difficulties at work, I began to realize I could still communicate with her on a different level. I understood we can still "talk to someone on the other side," which many call prayer. I asked my mom for guidance, for help, for support. Things I could not do when she was alive. We never had a great relationship. I was a tomboy and she wanted a prissy young lady who liked dolls, makeup and frilly things. As her eldest daughter, I was a great disappointment to her on this level yet a source of pride for my intellectual nature. So there was the rub.

During these nine months when I was finally intimately communicating with my mom, I literally thought I might lose my job. I began to pray in earnest for the first time in my life and realized I had brought all my problems with me from New Mexico. I hadn't escaped anything because all "the problems" were deep inside me; I knew I had to change from the inside out. The hymn, *Amazing Grace* became my theme song. I had a yearning I'd never recognized. It was a longing to be one with the Great Spirit who some call God, Mother, Father.

I was having a great deal of difficulty at work. It was the first time in my career that people didn't seem to like me. As a principal of an elementary school, there are many challenges, but none as difficult as having gossip and lies spread about you. I was devastated as I gradually found out the extent of the deception that was going on right under my nose. The gossip was so destructive because I didn't know the exact content of it and therefore it was extremely complex to counteract.

This chaos at work brought me to my knees as I began delving into various spiritual authors like Louise Hay, Wayne Dyer, Deepak Chopra, Caroline Myss, *A Course in Miracles* and many other similar works. I started looking in the mirror and wondering about past, present and future relationships. Of utmost importance was the relationship with my life partner whom I had left in Albuquerque. We had been together for 23 years and supported one another through many joys and sorrows with the help of our favorite friends like Jose Cuervo, Jim Beam, and Jack Daniels, among others. We'd drown our pains and celebrate our accomplishments, always with a bottle of something. Our intimacy was limited to times when we were drinking, which led to many conflicts and irrational behaviors. I drank to drown pain and sorrow and always felt I could control my drinking. I blamed him and decided I had enough of his drunkenness. He had the problem—not me.

After living in Arizona a few months I did stop drinking completely and started feeling a lot better. I changed my diet based on overhearing a conversation a teacher was having about her health problems, which were identical to mine. I was infested with candida and have since rid myself of it by eliminating sugar and flour from my diet. I began doing yoga and meditating after hitting bottom at work. I didn't turn to alcohol, as I would have in Albuquerque, so I *had* grown and started to appreciate inner strength because of my faith. I had searched for many years and yearned for this faith but had never really found it. After reading Brian Weiss' book, *Many Lives, Many Masters,* I began to realize the people in my life were here to help my soul get to the next level of consciousness. It wasn't about this life but it was about eternal life. My whole attitude about life was changing. My faith was taking on a new dimension. I was truly evolving into something different. I stopped watching television and started listening to uplifting music. Dr. Emoto and his work with water inspired me. On a much deeper level I started realizing that, as Louise Hay states, "Your thoughts create your experiences." Consciousness truly does determine your life, your health, and your very existence.

These insights are not my doing but truly the grace of God in my life. This divinity in me, in you, can be reached if we just look for it, it's there just waiting to be kindled. It is awe inspiring, uplifting and will get you through anything. I've learned to surrender through meditation and prayer, trusting that the beloved is always with me just waiting to help, to give me peace of mind. And every experience is a means to a higher level of consciousness, a sentinel for the soul.

I have encountered the divine in all the little everyday miracles in my life. My relationship with my life partner has changed because I have changed. I have a new sense of appreciation for all his good qualities and the lessons we're here to learn in this life together. We have been together before and if we don't get it right this time, we'll have more time together in another life to elevate our souls.

Love endures. Each of us is a holy child of God here to create a better world.

CONNECTING WITH OUR INNER POWER

Susanna Albuquerque, Portugal

*"I was rediscovering the holistic approach
to life and starting to understand that life's
unfair events have the purpose of teaching us
to love ourselves and each other more. . ."*

When I first met Isis we were both 14 and attending the same high school class. She was a warm, generous and light-hearted young woman. Born in one of the former Portuguese colonies in Africa, she kept the openness and strong energy of the vast steppe. She was a joyful inspiring friend who was always available and non-judgemental. After high school we went to different universities and eventually lost track of each other.

However, three years later I was informed that my good friend Isis had been in a train accident and as a result of it had lost her right leg. I was so shocked and angry with the "unnecessary punishment from life," that for many years I didn't have the courage to get in touch with her. I felt as though I had nothing to tell her. The whole thing was very hard for me to accept and mostly I thought it was unbearably unfair: how could life take away from such a wonderful human being the possibility of moving freely? How could life restrict her choices and possibilities in such a way?

Although I didn't get in touch with Isis, I kept following her achievements from a distance. After a year in Germany doing a series of treatments to ensure her recovery, she got a prosthesis, returned to Portugal, and graduated from Law School. After that she got a job as a legal expert at the Foreign Affairs Ministry where she pursued a brilliant career.

At the same time, I was rediscovering the holistic approach to life and starting to understand that life's unfair events have the purpose of teaching us to love ourselves and each other more. So, when I started accepting life's mysterious, though wise, events, I ran into my friend Isis on an island in the middle of the Atlantic. We were both attending the same conference! We just carried on from there as if no time had ever passed since the last time we had met.

Later my friend applied for and got a placement as a legal expert of the European Commission in Brussels. She told me then that she didn't know why she wanted to move alone to a foreign city where she'd hardly met anyone, but it was a gut feeling she had to follow. As my work required me to travel to Brussels 3 or 4 times a year, I started staying over at Isis' place.

Isis had developed an enormous strength, which she used solely for her successful professional activity but emotionally she felt scared, hopeless and her self-esteem was extremely low. She thought she only deserved to obtain professional goals through very hard work and effort and felt as if she didn't deserve to have an active social or emotional life.

At that time I had started using Louise Hay's methods and was telling Isis how much it had enabled me to recover my personal power and self-esteem. She immediately asked me to get her the *You Can Heal Your Life* book. As soon as Isis started reading the book she felt as if she had discovered gold! After so many years she realised she was still blaming herself for the accident.

She also learned she could free the victim in her by forgiving herself for having the accident which resulted in physical restriction and that she could now attract into her life everything she wanted by using affirmations.

When Isis started to forgive herself and to love and accept herself unconditionally everything around her started to change. She started to believe not only was she innocent but also that she deserved to improve her quality of life. Forgiveness and affirmations were, according to her, the keys.

For many years Isis had been told by doctors and prosthesis experts that it would be impossible to find her a better prosthesis –yet when she started doing affirmations saying that she would easily find a much better prosthesis that would improve her quality of life, the Universe moved to help her. She found an affordable center nearby. Although the first doctor she met there confirmed his previous colleagues opinion, she did not give up and kept affirming that she would easily find a technician who together with her would get her the best solution. And so they did! In less than one month they managed to get Isis a wonderful new prosthesis. The new prosthesis enabled her to do new things that were not possible before: to wear a skirt, take Yoga lessons, walk for longer periods, and even to have a much better posture.

Presently Isis is preparing for the exams to become an official of the European Commission. This involves a great amount of stress because there are 20,000 candidates for 200 vacancies. Yet as soon as she started using affirmations saying that she was divinely guided, the relevant information, courses and material were laid on her lap without any effort from her.

Isis has also realised that what was initially a strange foreign city has become her home, allowing her to find herself. She deeply believes in the power of affirmations to improve her life and is now starting to work with them for her social and emotional life. She's realised she shouldn't have to be limited to being a good professional only, but also deserves, as any other human being, a wonderful social and emotional life. I am pretty sure that the Universe is already conspiring to deliver her the best! She is ordering it!

The story of Isis and my own experience have demonstrated the truth of the Dali Lama's words:

"*We are gifted human beings with this wonderful human intelligence and all human beings have the capacity to be very determined and to direct that strong sense of determination in whatever direction they would like to use it.*"

By recognising our inner power we will no longer regard ourselves as victims of a forceful world. As we acknowledge our power we are able to start exercising it through affirmations and visualisations. These extremely simple tools will direct the Universe's energy to deliver us our soul wishes.

Most importantly, affirmations and visualisations enable us to raise our self-esteem and to strengthen our self-acceptance and unconditional love for ourselves and therefore for others. We then recognise and experience our true nature as divine beings that co-create our world on Earth.

HEALING FROM THE
INSIDE OUT
Georgina Agnew, Ireland

*"Many nights, weeks, months, were spent
releasing our anger, guilt, fear, resentment,
criticism and sense of duty..."*

At the age of thirty-eight I was bankrupt,
which wasn't well received by my family,
compounding the stigma that I was indeed
a failure. "Champagne tastes on a beer income" was
their war cry.

Health had always been in question: I had chronic
back pain throughout my nursing career and was an in-
sulin-dependent diabetic. My ethos: I had to work hard
to get anywhere, and needless to say, put in a ridiculous
number of shifts, working seven nights a week, blaming
my poor health for everything. In fact I just blamed everybody, and nothing was ever my fault. I was a frequent
recipient of my doctor's surgery, complaining of some
ailment or other, usually resulting in hospitalisation for
more surgery.

"Control freak" would be my most apt description,
as censure was high on my agenda—critical of others,
but even more critical of me. Nothing was ever good

enough and I certainly never reached the bench mark of perfection. At this stage I was popping 8-12 high strength prescription painkillers per day and more pills to get to sleep at night.

The only respite from my own self-imposed, miserable existence was that I had begun to attend a spiritualist church, which in turn led me to sit in a development circle affording the opportunity to explore and develop my mediumship.

My Mother passed in 1995 leaving a gaping hole in my life, the stress of which highlighted underlying problems in my marriage, culminating in a deepening rift between my husband and I. In 1996 I moved out of my marital home with my two children and went back to live with my Dad.

My career hit a very low ebb. I had taken my boss to a tribunal—a court of justice; and I may have won the battle but the war had just begun. Shortly afterward I spent the night with a colleague getting drunk, and we both laughed and joked about how we could push the boss under a bus. I vividly recall wishing I would never have to go back to work. As if by magic, the very next day I was the one who got knocked down by a car.

My injuries weren't critical but enough to secure yet another stay in hospital. Pain raged throughout my body, I had great difficulty walking and bending, and not even morphine injections could provide relief. Finally discharged with a diagnosis of a slipped disc, I returned home, where my condition deteriorated.

My difficulties compounded when my GP phoned and said that he urgently needed to speak to me. In his consulting room his words were "there is no easy way to tell you, so maybe it is better if you read the letter from the hospital yourself." I read, but without comprehension: "spine of a 65-year-old, arthritis throughout the body," and then the doctor dropped the bombshell: I would be in a wheelchair within two years. Stunned at this revelation, 90% of me was relieved; I wouldn't need to go back to work. The other 10% was in fear of the devastation this would cause to my finances.

My health continued to deteriorate, so much so that my husband moved in, as I was fully dependent on others to provide my basic care.

That year my Father suffered a brain hemorrhage. Against everyone's advice I brought him home, so there were now two of us who required nursing.

My Father survived for 3½ years. During this time I comforted myself by drinking over 4 litres of coca cola per day and manifested a cataract, adding to an ever-increasing list of complaints. Naturally, my body had become extremely incapacitated and I eventually took to a wheelchair. I was indeed a very disagreeable person: I shouted, screamed and made two attempts to end my life. My only relief was working with spirit.

In May 2000, two days before my birthday, events took a dramatic turn. A man jumped over the central barrier while I was travelling on a busy motorway and stood in my path. Unable to take evasive action, my car hit him, killing him instantly. This episode lead me to a psychiatrist, and this was good as I realised I didn't want to live my life this way any longer.

I found myself in a bookshop at the self-help section. *You Can Heal Your Life* by Louise Hay fell at my feet and some kind soul picked it up for me. Reading the cover, I knew I had to purchase the book together with its Companion Book. I read avidly, recording all 36 of my DIS-EASES.

After reading the book several times I tried some of the exercises; I lifted a mirror and couldn't get the words out: "I love and approve of myself." How could I love and approve of myself when I was seven stone (98 pounds) overweight? It was a shocking revelation to realise I was responsible for what had shown up in my life.

For the next few months I attempted to cut down my medication, and asked my parents for help via mediumship. Miraculously my wonderful friend, Alison, appeared. Like me, she was at a crossroads in her life and also reading *You Can Heal Your Life.* We decided to facilitate for each other trying to source the root causes of our ailments. Many nights, weeks, months, were spent releasing our anger, guilt, fear, resentment, criticism and sense of duty. We listed all our diseases and said the appropriate affirmations. It seemed to be never-ending; the more we did, the more we had to do. The amazing result was the more we let go of these emotions and belief patterns, the more our bodies responded, becoming more flexible and pain-free.

I had started to shed some of my cumbersome weight and was able to walk totally unaided. Feeling so good, I told the medical profession what I was doing and asked if I could come off insulin. This was met by stark astonishment; in their opinion I was heading for disaster. Furthermore, I was made to sign a form exonerating the hospital of any responsibility. Undeterred, I stopped taking insulin to root out the cause of the diabetes. My weight dropped dramatically.

Alison and I were both at a place where we knew *You Can Heal Your Life* had influenced our lives so dramatically that we wished to progress to helping others. We were fortunate enough to meet Patricia and Rick when we went to the United States to train as facilitators for Heal Your Life Workshops.

This was the next step in my development and yet another journey of self-discovery. The training was filled with many valuable exercises to unravel even more limiting belief systems. Returning home armed with this knowledge I continued to realise my true potential and finally discarded my 18-year addiction to sleeping pills.

I even lost my attachment to Scotland, my country of birth, and moved to Ireland. I was inspired to work with horses, a true passion of mine, and now have the ability to ride my own horse, the realisation of a childhood dream.

The opportunity has also arisen to offer workshops and seminars for holistic therapists using Louise's book. The aim is to help them understand the gravity of the mind/body connection, which in turn produces a more complete profile of their client, creating a new dimension to work during treatments. Ultimately, I feel compelled to enlighten people that the power to heal lies within.

It is with gratitude to Louise and her wonderful words that my life is full of vitality, purpose and vibrant health. At the age of 50, I take full responsibility for everything that shows up in my life. Of course I'm still learning. The difference now is that I have the tools to help myself manifest the life I love.

Anyone can heal their life if they really want to.

THE POWER OF THE
UNCONSCIOUS MIND
Patricia Crane, Ph.D., California

*"I subtly learned we couldn't afford what we
really wanted because it cost too much. . ."*

During my college years an incident occured
that taught me a powerful lesson about the
unconscious mind and how it can sabatoge
one's ability to create what you want. Prior to the start
of each new college year, my mother would take me
shopping for clothes. Just before my senior year we
went shopping as usual. I needed a new coat, and it
had to be a warm one because my college was near
Chicago, Illinois, and the winters were really cold. On
this particular shopping day, I saw the most beautiful
coat I had ever seen. It was camel colored, long, warm
and fit perfectly. <u>And</u> it was on sale. But even on sale
it was more than Mom would have normally spent for
me on clothes, and we still had more shopping to do.
She looked at my face and saw how much I wanted that
coat, smiled, and took it to the counter to pay for it. I
was so excited! This stunning coat was perfect.

A week later I was on a flight from Newark, New Jersey to the Chicago airport. There was so much to pack I carried my raincoat and my beautiful new coat. Once in Chicago, two friends and I hailed a cab to take us to the college housing. With three of us, we were tightly packed in the back of the cab, and so my coats went up behind the seat. When we arrived at the college, we all piled out and started taking our suitcases upstairs. About fifteen minutes later, I suddenly realized I had left my coats in the cab! Feeling panicked, I couldn't even remember the name of the cab company, and neither could my friends. I started calling companies in the phone book, asking if any of their cabbies had reported the forgotten coats. No, no, no. I felt devastated. How would I tell Mom the expensive coat was lost? Why had I been so dumb as to lose it? I mentally berated myself for being so careless. And I had so looked forward to wearing that beautiful coat.

Years later, when I began studying how old negative beliefs limit us and how to use affirmations to counteract them and thus create a different life, I finally understood why I had "unconsciously" forgotten the coat. When I was growing up, I was taught to believe, "you can have nice things, but not what you REALLY want because it's too expensive." In our middle-class home we always had enough to eat, dressed nicely, and had a comfortable environment, yet I subtly learned we couldn't afford what we really wanted because it cost too much. The coat had been what I really wanted, and that was opposite my belief, so my unconscious mind managed to help me prove the old belief by losing the coat before I even wore it. When I realized that, I could stop blaming myself for the loss. Forgiveness was easy. My new affirmation became "I deserve to receive exactly what I want and I have plenty of money to pay for it."

Now when some challenge happens, I take time in meditation to discover what unconscious belief might be lurking that has created a situation I didn't want on the conscious level. Once I can identify the old belief, I can begin to claim a new belief using affirmations and visualization.

The unconscious mind carries ALL of our beliefs about every area of life: relationships, success, career, self-esteem, health, etc. These beliefs are constantly creating our lives, yet most people are completely unaware of the power of the unconscious. If you are unhappy with some area of your life, begin to examine what you were taught growing up. Some of the messages might have been overt, while others were subtle. Once you become aware of the limiting beliefs, you can begin to use tools like affirmations and visualizations to change them and create the life you really want.

Re-Entering the Soul

Barbara Avril Burgess, England

*"All my relatives behaved in their way because
that was 'all they knew and understood'. . ."*

I have a family photo of my Grandmother. She is
the smallest, scruffiest and unhappiest person
in the picture. What made her that way?

She met my Grandfather when he was living in Dr.
Barnardo's home. She passed the home each day on
her way to school and they would talk to each other
through the railings. I don't know why he was there; in
my grandfather's day people would put their children
in a home if they couldn't afford to keep them. These
places were very 'cold' emotionally and regimentally
run.

My father was bullied at school, and Grandfather
told him to fight those who bullied him, so my father
grew up a very hard and angry man. His mother locked
him out of the house each day and although she bought
him things, she never gave them to him; just put them
away in a cupboard. When she died we found brand

new buckets and spades for the seaside and brand new children's clothes still in their shop wrappers. Perhaps she bought the tin bucket and spade in the hopes of going to the seaside but in the end couldn't afford the holiday. Who knows?

What happened in my relatives' lives to make them behave like they did? Psychologists say that all our behaviour is learned behaviour. I grew up a very unhappy child, teenager and adult as a result of being bullied both mentally and physically by my parents, school children, and other children in the 'rough' neighbourhood where we lived. My father would punch us three children on our arm, enough to send us backwards, whilst he shouted in our face. I also remember him hitting my sister so much and for so long one night, I thought he would never stop.

He shouted from morning to night. He shouted if the sun was shining and he shouted if it was raining; he shouted because his dinner was too hot or too cold and would often throw it against the wall or turn the plate over onto the table cloth. One day when mother was ill, he threw the sugar bowl at her. So I grew up a very unhappy and angry person, and hated the world. The only things I loved were animals in general and dogs in particular.

What changed my life was meeting Patricia Crane and taking the *Heal Your Life* course. I don't even know why I did; it was as if I was 'pushed' to do it. I booked at the last minute; in fact I only discovered it a few days before and somehow the money for it came at the same time.

That week was the most wonderful week of my life and the fabulous people I met there and the course changed my life completely. During that week the one statement that 'hit' me right in the face was 'with the knowledge and understanding that a person has at the time.' I then realised my parents and their parents and their parents before them behaved the way they did because they only had the 'knowledge and understanding' to behave in that way at that time. The two words go together, 'knowledge and understanding.' All my relatives behaved in their way because that was 'all they knew and understood.'

During the *Heal Your Life* course I laughed a lot, cried a lot and hugged a lot. I had not known how to hug before that! I did a lot of forgiving too. I listened to Louise Hay's tape on anger and dealt with so much anger towards my parents and other people in my life. Again I cried and punched a lot of cushions and pillows! I realised that some of the anger was directed at people I *thought* I was angry at. This, too, was an eye opener. Sometimes we blame certain people for things when in fact it is another person who is to blame. The Louise Hay tape brought this message home to me. I did a lot of work on healing the child within and forgave myself too.

My father left my mother when I was 16; I am now in my 60th year. At that time he moved to Africa and I thought I would never see him again. Although he treated us roughly, we still loved him and he did have his gentle side, although it only showed on rare occasions. He was very strong, and I remember one day in the garden, he picked all three of us children up in his arms at the same time and we thought he was as strong as the famous 'Tarzan'. He loved nature and animals and he often brought home a sick bird that he had found in the road that may have been hit by a car. He also had a sense of humour and managed to laugh on odd occasions. He was a very clever man and could build a glider without using any plans. He just 'knew' how to do it.

When he left for Africa we all said our farewells and cried a lot. The next day he turned up again shouting because he had forgotten something. We felt cheated, because we had believed he was leaving and had all said our sad goodbyes and then the next day he turned up on our doorstep, his usual bullying self.

When his mother died some 10 years later he came back to England, and we were glad to see him even if it was a sad time. In his usual way he conned us and tricked us and made us feel unhappy, but nevertheless we were sad to see him leave once more. During yet another tearful goodbye he said "I have no reason to come back to England now that my mother is dead." I remember thinking: *What about me, dad? What about your three children?*

I was very hurt and very angry. Regularly my sister, brother and I wrote our dad hate mail! I told him he could have changed and he could have learned, but then I didn't know of that phrase 'knowledge and understanding'. He simply did not know how to change or even that he could.

He returned to England four years ago. I didn't make contact with him until after doing the *Heal Your Life* course. Then, at Christmas 2004, my elder daughter helped me find him, and on Christmas Eve we met. (Unbeknown to either of us he had moved near where I live.) We knocked on his door, we hugged and we cried; I hugged his 5th wife. (I get on very well with her; she is the same age as my elder daughter and my dad is 84!) Dad came round for Christmas lunch; his wife declined as she said it would be best for us all to get to know Dad again without her and as they had just moved in there was much unpacking to do.

I get on really well with dad now. We hug and kiss hello and goodbye and I can see by his face that he welcomes this. I listen to his moans and groans, and accept him now for who he is. He talks about the war and how he hated it and how he and the German soldiers he made friends with, at great risk to himself, just wanted to get on with their own lives, working and earning money for their families. He told me how he had helped 30 German people, men, women and children, who were living in a cow barn and were covered in fleas, lice and sores and had very little food to survive. Officers had commandeered their homes. He stole bandages and cream and some food to give to them and bribed both English and German soldiers on guard so that he could take the stuff to the farm. He did this at great risk to himself but it shows that he's a kind and gentle person really; it's just that what happens to you in life can change you.

So this is where forgiveness really counts and especially those special words 'knowledge and understanding'. If we use our knowledge and understanding that people act the way they do because of their 'knowledge and understanding', we can be ready to forgive anyone.

NATURE IS OUR GUIDE

Chantal Clearwater, Australia

*"The guardian of the door to your heart is yourself.
You are free to unlock it at any moment. . ."*

Whilst walking in the bush I noticed a very small but exquisite and delicate purple flower. It was its' delicate and easily missed beauty that led to my mind being impressed with the following message. I believe it was not meant for me alone. I wrote down these words as Spirit spoke to me:

> You are like a small, delicate, yet exquisitely
> beautiful and rare purple flower. None other
> of its kind in the world, growing behind
> and shaded by a large rock up the top of a
> mountain, where no one can see it. Those
> who stumble upon its unique beauty are
> rewarded in the treasure found.
>
> Use this knowledge wisely.
> Be guided.

Be not afraid, for you are protected by the
golden sword and the all-pervading light of
truth and love.
I love you and serve you.

Use the tools I have given you.
Love serves all.
Love serves self and others.
I serve you because you serve me.
You are my delicate flower.
Open up to your true beauty and potential.

Don't make a slave of yourself serving the
foolish ego and not me.
I love you.
Surrender your heart to the Lord above,
merge with The Oneness and The Light.
Let go to Love, it will guide you.
It will serve you well.

All is yours out of the great love I have for
you and all my children.
All is ours to share in benediction and love
and blessings, kindly embracing each other
with our united hearts' embrace.

Sweet, delicate, blossoming one
—struggle not, but flow.
The gushing tide cannot be stopped
with fear or grief or restlessness
but will take us on to new pastures and valleys,
and will flow into new rivers.

The tides of love carry you not because I wish
to thwart you but because you are young and
growing and have not the wisdom to see with
clarity the things I see and know.

Love is my hand.
Take it and walk with me, our hearts united.
Together we will soar free on wings of love.
Loves sweet embrace, loves tender, exotic
fragrance, dewdrops of joy and peace, they
are yours and they are mine if you are willing
to accept and be led by me.
Joy, freedom, peace, love and bliss
—bathe in the sunlight of these heartfelt
emotions—my heartfelt promise to you.

All are found in silence, in prayer, in praise,
in giving and loving, yet one must risk in
order to be free.
One must risk and one must give to have.
One must go out on a limb, put oneself (the
ego) last in order to be first with me.
I love you, you are free, you have worked
hard and I carry you on eagle's wings.
Peace is yours if you trust me completely.

The guardian of the door to your heart is
yourself.
You are free to unlock it at any moment.
Come, travel, see, and shine.
Power and wisdom are yours.
Do not be afraid.
I love you.

I love you so much I give all of myself to you.
This I ask of you—to give all of yourself to
me and all of yourself to my family.
Our sweet embrace will be pure ecstasy, the
joy of being.
Do not hold back out of fear.
You are protected and will not be harmed.

Nor can you go astray unless you stray from me.

This is why it is so important to be clear, to have clarity so that you can see and feel my guiding hand leading you, and so you do not mistake it. The blind often falter through lack of faith and trust because they do not recognise me and so fear me.

Fear not.
There is nothing to fear, you are safe with me.
Don't be fooled into thinking there are evils out to harm you.
They are my battle not yours.
You do yourself the greatest harm.

Innocence, not naivety or ignorance, is a rare quality in today's world.
Nurture your innocence, it is your beauty.
You are my child, my beloved child.
Don't try to make anything happen yourself.
Just trust in me that all will be well.
I will guide your steps.
Keep close to me.

You are free.
You are loved and you are cherished.

It is your innocence and playfulness, Chantal, that you need to tune into for this is what you will impart to/teach others. This joy of the child trusting implicitly in Love—The Father/ Mother God) you will give to others, enticing them to reach into themselves and tune into their own playfulness and innocence, reaching into and gaining strength from their own vulnerability.

The vulnerable will be protected because they have the most to give. They do not close it away, hiding and protecting their treasure so that no one can share in it. They give freely and willingly. Sure, they may have been hurt very badly. It is through their courage to be willing to open up again and risk it all, that they will be rewarded abundantly.

The world is a beautiful place.
In your eyes is a sunrise; in your heart a rainbow of colours; in your smile is the laughter of many.

In your eyes shines the soul of the earth and in your tears is the gentle mourning of God.
The entire world is a beautiful place.
Shine your colours, your rainbow colours for all to see.
On your face are a sunset and a moonrise.
On the shores of your soul are the colours of the rainbow, the rainbow of all the colours, united and strong.

You are an instrument of peace;
an instrument of love.
Find your own unique voice;
your own unique colours;
your true, heartfelt presence.

Look within; I reside in your heart,
in 'the heart' of truth.

Follow your heart day-to-day,
moment-to-moment.
All we have is now.
We cannot know what the future will bring,
let alone the next moment.
Contemplate nature to understand this.
Cycles; seasons; change; are the only things of
which we can be sure.

Life is too precious to waste. How often do we take
the time and make the effort to notice the gifts and intuit
the guidance nature has for us? How many of us walk
past or even step on that little, exquisite purple flower
that is so unique and rare and holds a treasure trove of
wisdom; the eternal truths of existence? Love, beauty and
truth—it is there all around us, within us and within all
things. Are we too busy, acting out our own dramas and
focusing on the negative that we become blind to the
real beauty of the world, each other and ourselves? We
are interconnected with all things, and nature is there
to guide us and teach us how to live. Listen with your
heart. Allow the still timelessness and beauty to pervade
your consciousness. The gifts are all there if we open to
receive them!

–**Excerpted from** *Seeds Of Unconditional Love*

NEVER GIVE UP!

Mardi Zeunert, Australia

*"During this time, I discovered the biggest thing
I needed to do was forgive myself and the people
who had come into all stages of my life. . ."*

Although I had a relatively carefree childhood in South Australia, I was instructed
that *'children should be seen and not heard'* and
'be thankful for what you have in life; don't ask for more.' Shy,
I found it hard to communicate what I wanted.

My family moved to the country and then back
to the city when I was 16. It was a tough age grappling
with my identity; the city girls were so cool, and I felt
unfashionable. I started smoking and pretending to be
like them while floundering at school, believing I wasn't
good at anything as I kept failing math. It was apparent I
was only skillful at typing, so I left school and my parents
enrolled me in a secretarial course. I never questioned
their decision, nor even knew what other options were
available.

Until my adult years I found those early messages
still holding a firm grip . . . for the inability to speak up,
I sometimes paid a price. *Can you really have it all - and*

190

more? I never thought when I was a teenager that life would take so many twists and turns.

On completion of the secretarial course, I was offered a role as a receptionist and worked hard for a promotion to secretary. *"That's all I ever want to be,"* I'd say; it was true, for I had no idea there was more to life and more to me . . . By 19 I believed that having a man in my life would now make my life complete.

At 20 I became engaged. He was 'tall, dark and handsome' . . . *the one.* When he called our wedding off just before my 21st birthday, I felt like a part of me died—I was a failure.

My first introduction to a self-help book came from my understanding personnel manager, who took me to a bookshop; we bought a book about love and loss. The book and her encouraging words helped me understand what had happened. It became bearable when I finally started to communicate, asking questions, listening, talking about how I felt.

After grieving and feeling left out as all my friends were getting married, I soon proudly declared again that I'd finally met *'the right one'* and was going to get married. I was 22. Recalling our wedding day and the pangs of doubt in my stomach, I now know I realized then that this marriage wouldn't be the fairytale union I'd yearned for. My husband was a drinker and couldn't cope with alcohol, causing some terrible public embarrassments. Accompanying the abuse of his own body was the mental abuse hurled at me during his benders. Others could see how much damage the relationship was doing to me, but I was in denial—clinging to the hope that things weren't as bad as they seemed.

During the next five years of marriage I became very independent. I left my job and moved to another company and was promoted into a marketing role. Despite this professional confidence in my abilities, my own life in the shadows of self-doubt left me thinking I didn't deserve such a good job. After all, I hadn't even finished high school and didn't have a university degree.

Hurt and worn down by the tumult of my dysfunctional marriage, I began to engage in the blame game; blaming him for our strained relationship and bringing his problems into my life. Determined not to fail, I resolved to put all my energy into trying to change him. He rebelled to my controlling ways, and things got worse. Finally, I summoned the courage to leave.

After wrestling with the guilt of having abandoned him, I started to realise that I was letting *myself* down by not being true to who I was. I started to ask myself the hard questions: where was my self-love, and how could I love another if I didn't love myself? The overwhelming internal message: I was a failure, engaged twice, married once and divorced at 25.

Only when I truly realised I was part of the cycle, always picking the same type of people in relationships, looking to others for my own happiness, and letting others make decisions for me, did I begin to take some responsibility.

But then I brushed these realisations aside when another man came along who told me he was *'the one and only'* and promised me the perfect life. I felt he would save me and we'd live happily ever after. I became engaged for the third time, and had a huge one-carat diamond to prove it. But while my so-called fairytale life had a shiny veneer, I knew it was a lie. I used to hide my ring when I was wearing it.

It was the beginning of a two-year nightmare of mental and violent physical abuse; my body told me 'no more' when cancerous cells were discovered in my cervix. Fortunately, with treatment this wasn't life threatening.

Then I faced the cold, hard truth: I was in my husband's house, curled up in a fetal position, in poor health with bruises on my body, struggling with anti-depressant medication, no job, car, money, or home of my own; no friends or family around and only the woman on the end of the phone at Lifeline.

It took this horrendous, frightening experience in which I hit rock bottom, in order for me to make the break. After feeling I'd lost everything, I said, *no more!* I rang my mum who came and collected me, and told her the truth.

Around this time, loving people who looked at life differently from the perspective that I'd had started entering my life. After many spirited conversations, listening to their stories, spending time alone, and visits to the bookshop, I slowly started tapping into the answers within. I listened to myself and trusted my decisions, finally reaching a turning point at 30.

During this time, I discovered the biggest thing I needed to do was forgive myself and the people who had come into all stages of my life. I started trusting who I wanted to be, and kept reminding myself to keep talking and listening in a positive and powerful way.

After getting back on my feet and feeling self-love for the first time, I was offered a marketing job in the UK. While waiting for an overseas work visa I met my beautiful future husband. I felt I had come a long way in my own personal development. The challenge: *could life be this good?* I asked myself, *is it for real, will he treat me well, and do I want to marry again? Could I be blessed in having children?*

I questioned his love and desire to spend his life with me. He told me he was speaking his truth from the heart and that was all he could do. So I let go of my old stories and trusted, forgiving myself for negative questioning. I knew life was different because I was different. My affirmations for a wonderful life filled with love and truth had worked. We married and I stayed in Australia.

My working career then took off in many wonderful directions as well. I reflected on where I had come in my career, and decided I wanted to tread another journey. My new learned wisdom and self-love helped me create a new career, and give me confidence to take risks. The more I opened up my heart and spoke my truth, the more opportunities came my way.

I understand now that people come into our lives for a reason, and teach us valuable lessons. They have shown me how I want to live my life, who I want to be, and what I don't want. I'm finally able to thank them for being a part of my life.

I truly believe the wisdom in the saying that '*life is a journey only you can lead.*' What the future holds is up to us, and the only way to predict the future is to create it. The biggest keys of all are to love ourselves, stay true, forgive and give thanks to the beautiful people in our lives. Life is for living.

THE TREASURE IN THE HAT
Rick Nichols, California

*"To my shock he lifted the hat from his
head and held it high in the air. . . ."*

It had been approaching dusk on a warm summer day in Surf City, USA. Strolling along the beach enjoying the feel of the warm sand on my bare feet and squinting against the bright setting sun, I could scarcely make out the silhouette of a man walking towards me. While passing to my left the man stopped suddenly, turned and touched my shoulder.

"Hey, are you from Huntington Beach?" he asked with a bright, friendly smile.

One would think that would be an easy question to answer, but being somewhat taken aback by his sudden and direct approach I had to ponder the question for a moment. He waited patiently, smiling cheerfully while I thought it over.

"Uh, why yes, yes I guess I am." I stammered.

"Well then, you need a hat!" he declared. (He was wearing a ball cap with the words Huntington Beach,

Surf City, USA, and a surfer riding a wave, embroidered on it.)

With that he suddenly reached up, grabbed the bill of his cap, removed it from his head, and placed it securely on mine. All at once I was filled with anger and fear. I felt rudely violated and compelled to lash out at this kindly fellow who was standing there still grinning from ear to ear. Fortunately, I checked these strange emotions, said thank you, and removed the hat as I walked away.

Where the devil did that come from? I wondered. *Why react so strongly and negatively to this simple act of kindness?*

Replaying the scene over and over in my mind for the next several days I searched for the source of this irrational response that had been so easily triggered. This was a period in my life when I had been doing a lot of "soul searching." Until the previous year, life had consisted of just rambling around from job to job and relationship to relationship trying to do and be what I thought others expected me to do and be. Over the long haul it hadn't worked out too well.

One of the more important lessons learned up to that point in my searching was that there are no coincidences, everything has a purpose, and every "chance" encounter offers another piece of the puzzle of life. I knew this encounter on the beach was far more than it appeared to be, and that the hat was more than an ordinary ball cap.

Dropping off to sleep a few nights later, an old memory flashed back. I was at school in the first grade and there was an epidemic of head lice and ringworm going around. School administrators had sent out flyers admonishing parents to tell their children to:

NEVER WEAR ANOTHER'S HAT OR USE ANOTHER'S BRUSH OR COMB

. . . as these practices spread the diseases.

My mother was a single mom with three children. It was tough to get by and she worked hard to provide for our basic needs; there would be very little money for doctor visits. Additionally, a stigma that went along with ringworm and head lice at the time was that most people who contracted the infections were "unclean" or lived in unclean conditions. Mom would be most unhappy to imagine the neighbors and others whispering rumors that we were unclean—perish the thought. She made it dreadfully clear to me and my siblings that to come home with one or both of these diseases would elicit the most severe of reprimands. I believed her.

Also, part of the treatment for ringworm was to shave the infected head, quite fashionable for men and boys in today's world, but certainly not in 1953, and I did feel a strong need to look cool. Once they got your head shaved, bright orange medication was put on the infected areas, definitely not cool. Finally, and this was the worst of it all, they would cut the foot off of a woman's nylon stocking (these were pre-pantyhose times), tie a large knot in the calf section, slip it on your head, and make you wear the dreadful thing—everywhere you went!!! I don't know—maybe it prevents the bugs from head-hopping or something, but whatever the reasons, going around wearing my mother's underwear on my head was not the fashion statement I was willing to make, nor did it fit the image I was trying to create. The whole concept was unacceptable as far as I was concerned, and scared the dickens out of me even at the tender age of six.

Bingo! The lights came on! This incident at school all the way back when I was six years old, more than forty years earlier, was the reason I had reacted so strongly when the man on the beach put his hat on my head. It explained a lot about why I'd always been uncomfortable around hats, brushes and combs that don't belong to me. Unbeknownst to my conscious mind, for more than four decades, I had been harboring a belief that hats, combs and brushes belonging to other people are EXTREMELY DANGEROUS; I had a great-unknown fear of them! WOW- this hat did contain a wonderful treasure, a forgotten part of me.

Nevertheless, I wasn't so sure I liked this "treasure" because it came wrapped in a silly yet powerful fear that seemed to be tarnishing my self-esteem. I wanted to shove it back in the hat. Once out of the hat though, it wouldn't go back. I was stuck with it, but as I worked toward acceptance, I began to realize that it was just trying to protect me.

This experience revealed to me a "transparent" core belief I held. We all have many of them and we respond unconsciously to daily events through them. This particular belief (hats are dangerous) is fairly benign, it doesn't really matter if I wear someone else's hat or not. But it led me to ferret out other transparent beliefs that had actually been crippling me. As a result of being raised in a dysfunctional family, I discovered that I held powerful negative transparent beliefs about: men, women, marriage, family, children, work, play, money, education, right, wrong, good, bad, God, and myself—virtually everything about life that is important. I had actually built my life around these erroneous belief systems. No wonder it hadn't been working! The great gift in the hat was the discovery of these beliefs and subsequent freedom from them.

By the way, just discovering these beliefs doesn't make them go away. Several years ago I shared this story with a group of participants in a Salvation Army Rehabilitation program. As I was finishing the story a man in the front row began to move. This startled me a bit because he hadn't moved as much as a millimeter in the hour that I'd been speaking. I assumed he'd had a long night and was catching up on his sleep. I stepped back and watched as he slowly took hold of the bill of the ball cap he was wearing. To my shock he lifted the hat from his head and held it high in the air. He did all this without even looking up form his resting place on the table. His message was clear, "How do feel about this fine piece of head wear Bucko?"

Oh, whoops! I could have gone all day without seeing that hat offered up. I don't know where he got it, but I can assure you this hat had been around the block a few times. No telling what sort of microorganisms had taken up residence in there. Suddenly my tamed-down little belief about hats and their hazards, morphed into a winged fire-breathing daemon, complete with scales and a forked tail, squawking, shrieking and screaming, "Don't touch! Don't go near! Disease is imminent, run! Run! Run! Run for your life!" The old flee or fight response in its entire splendor was blooming big, and I was feeling the pressure.

I stood staring at the menacing hat. *Do I ignore it? Do I say thank you, end the program, and go home?* (I was almost out of time anyway.) Or do I step up to the beast and take it in hand? Taking a big deep breath and releasing it, I walked over to the man, took his hat and said "Thank you." Then, with a cocky little flair, plopped it on to my head and struck a pose, while reciting a silent prayer that I would not faint or die. Of course, no harm came to me. Quite the contrary, actually great things happened: the man offering the hat finally woke up (he demanded his hat back), I got a great round of applause and encouragement from the group, and I finally managed to satisfy that nagging little fear.

Still . . . whenever I come into proximity with another's hat, comb or brush I always hear that old alarm quietly ringing in the back of my mind. It's still with me but we're good friends now, and have learned to cohabitate peacefully.

More Pearls of Wisdom?

Do you have a story to tell?

Here is Your Opportunity to Become a Published Author!

If you are like most people the chances are very good that you have some pearls of wisdom that you need to dislodge from within and share with others. There is a wonderful healing quality in people's stories both for the storyteller and the receiver.

Pearls of Wisdom: A Second Strand, is already in the making. In fact the response has been so strong that we have a wait-list for a third release. We plan on publishing up to three more *Pearls of Wisdom* this year. Contact us now to reserve your chapter in an upcoming edition.

All you need to do is write your story, something inspiring, uplifting or humorous for people to enjoy. Perhaps a story that led you to a healing of body, mind or spirit, or something that touched you deeply enough that it compels you to share it with others. If the situation or event touched you, it is sure to reach out to others. Keep your story between 600 and 1200 words, and in English. Contact us now to assure your chapter in an upcoming *Pearls of Wisdom.*

For complete information and to download an application to send with your story go to:
www.HeartInspired.com/Pearls.pdf

Or contact us today for more information:
Heart Inspired Presentations
P.O. Box 1081, Bonsall, CA 92003
Tel: 760-728-8783 Fax: 760-728-7390
E-mail: Pearls@HeartInspired.com

Contributing Authors:

Georgina A. Agnew: Founder of Redwing Centre in Ireland, Georgina offers unique demonstrations of her mediumship to audiences worldwide. Georgina and colleague Alison provide inspirational workshops specifically designed for holistic therapists. These evolutionary seminars create new levels of understanding by promoting the mind-body connection and therefore empower people to make positive changes in their lives. All workshops are available nationally and internationally. Visit her web site at www.redwingcentre.com for further information and contact details.

Susana Albuquerque: Susana is a Personal Transformation Teacher, developing and conducting courses and workshops on Personal Development, Prosperity, Success, and Artistic and Creative Development. Susana is a qualified drama teacher, produces a monthly TV show and carries out her acting career on TV, Stage and Cinema, both in national and international productions. Susana is developing and managing projects of corporate social responsibility regarding financial education in Portugal. Fluent in Portuguese, Spanish, English and French, she is available to carry out workshops in any of these languages. For information please contact her on (351) 91 925 18 40. e-mail: s.albuquerque@asfac.pt

Erica Ashforth: Erica is a personal coach, mentoring teens and adults. She has been a motivational speaker for over 20 years, speaking to teens and as a spokesperson for Adult Children of Alcoholics. She leads transformational workshops and does destiny and relationship readings and reports. Her focus is on empowering individuals to create the life and relationships they desire. For further information and her upcoming web site please contact her by e-mail at ToCreateYourLife@aol.com. She is located in Henderson, Nevada and is available to travel for speaking and workshops. She is also available by phone for coaching and readings.

Barbara Badolati: Founder of Alive and Well in 1987, Barbara has guided thousands of people in experiencing greater health, balance and well-BEbeing. Barbara is a certified and licensed WellCoach™, yoga instructor and consultant for worksite health promotion. Her expertise has resulted in appearances on television, radio interviews, and feature writing in nationally syndicated papers. Barbara has produced several guided relaxation audio programs, which you can purchase on her web site, as well as learn more about her keynotes, workshops or WellCoaching sessions. Also sign up for her FREE monthly Well-BEing Tips. Visit: www.aliveandwellbarb.com or call (616) 638-5625.

SHARLENE BAUER: As a workshop facilitator and corporate trainer for over twenty years, Sharlene works with clients throughout the United States and Canada. She is committed to helping people overcome their fears of change, improve their communication skills, and enhance their self-confidence. Believing that "Sharing from the heart is the path to unity and peace in the world," she is available for inspiring and life-changing workshops. She is located in Escondido, CA and is available to travel to your city. Contact her at sharlenebauer@cox.net or call (760) 613-6522.

RENEE BECK: A Somatic Respiratory Integration (SRI) Facilitator, Renee is in the process of opening a healing center. She hosts retreats, workshops, and monthly full moon circles. For more information visit http://holistichands.abmp.com or call (607) 423-1743. She is located in Cortland, NY and is available to travel to other cities to offer workshops.

LAURINA BERGQVIST: A home schooling mother of 4 creative sons, Laurina divides her time between her summer home in southern Sweden and winters in Arizona. Visit her web site at www.geocities.com/lobergqvist to view samples of her artwork and learn more about the spirit dolls she loves to create. She holds a variety of creative and healing workshops for a wide range of ages. For information on upcoming workshops, please e-mail Laurina at lobergqvist@yahoo.com. Laurina has worked as a professional storyteller, and is available for storytelling in the U.S. and Sweden.

NAOMI BLAKE: Naomi's business is called The Light Within, because she really enjoys helping others find their inner light, and become empowered and fulfilled. Having finished her Masters of Counselling (phew!) and trained with leading mind/body experts such as Bernie Siegel, Patricia Crane, and Niravi Paine, she's creating a centre for mind/body work in Brisbane, Australia. Naomi offers counselling, workshops, meditation and fertility support. To find out more about the Blake ethos, and how to have your own 'aha' moments, visit her at www.geckohouse.com.au or call on (61) 0438626642.

CANDY BRADSHAW: Intuitive knowledge since childhood has led Candy to the fulfillment of her life's destiny, to be a teacher of Conscious Creation. Candy devotes her energy to communicating her ideals through seminars and personal coaching on Psicanica, a philosophy of spiritual development and self-discovery. Candy lives in the awareness that we all share a divine relationship with the universe; that we are the Creators of our own realities and life will manifest itself as we believe it will. For information on Psicanica products or to request a seminar in your area visit www.psicanica.com. Candy can be contacted at candy-bradshaw@psicanica.com.

BARBARA BURGESS: Writer, poet, psychic, medium and therapist, Barbara is trained in several of the new energy healing techniques as well as being a Reiki Master and counsellor. She is also a Heal Your Life, Achieve Your Dreams workshop leader. Visit her web site at www.yourbeautifulmind.com for more information. Barbara lives in Nottinghamshire, England and can be reached by e-mail at barbara@yourbeautifulmind.com. Barbara is a great lover of nature and animals, especially dogs. She is a great believer in people helping and empowering themselves and achieving their true potential through personal development.

BARBARA BURKE: As a versatile, enthusiastic training professional and human performance consultant, Barbara has over 20 years of experience as a computer user interface designer and facilitator of personal and business skill improvement courses. She is a certified Heal Your Life, Achieve Your Dreams teacher of transformational workshops. Through workshops and personal coaching, she loves helping people to increase their self-awareness, self-acceptance, and effectiveness in their daily life. Contact Barbara at barbara@barbaraburkeconsulting.com.

CHANTAL CLEARWATER: Chantal is a writer with a vision she calls "Seeds Of Unconditional Love", (SOUL), her business name. In 1993, she began 'receiving' pieces of the vision and segments of the book which she considers a large part of her life purpose. When she finishes collating her book, which she is also doing for children, Chantal would like to run "SOUL" personal and spiritual growth workshops. She is a Personal Coach, is studying to be a Science Of Life Counsellor and writes songs. Look out for her web site in the future. E-mail: seedsofunconditionallove@yahoo.com.au or phone: (mob): 0427556678. Cygnet, TAS, Australia.

LOTTIE DEVONTREE: In the dry and windy desert of Lethbridge, Alberta, Canada, Lottie has surrendered willingly to the daily catharsis of writing. This is where she also combines an odd pair of private practices: counseling with individuals and groups and the honor of living out the metaphor as a foot care specialist. An "outward expression of the inward harmony of the soul," says William Hazlitt. She is fortunate to be surrounded by amazing teachers, Prem Rawat, Gillian, her daughter, Joseph (her partner), delicious friends and relatives. e-mail: devgas@la.shockware.com

REV. CHRISTINE GREEN: The founding minister of Sacred Heart Ministries in Portland, Oregon, Rev. Green is an ordained minister and spiritual director serving her clients through classes, workshops and personal counseling. Her ministry was founded on a vision for helping others, especially women, incorporate Universal Truth into their professional and personal lives. To receive spiritual tools to support everyday living, the latest schedule of classes, or find out how to utilize her services as spiritual director, visit her web site at www.sacredheartministries.org or call 503-281-6301.

ANNE HARTLEY: Anne is the author of four books: *Love The Life You Live, Life Lessons, Love Your Money Love Your Life* and *The Psychology of Money.* Anne also works as a life coach and trains others to be life coaches using her values-based approach. She lives and works on the northern beaches of Sydney, Australia and coaches and trains students by phone anywhere in the world. If you would like to receive her free newsletter you can visit Anne's web site at www.hartlifecoaching.com.au or write to Anne at P. O. Box 769, Mona Vale, NSW 2103 Australia.

MICHAELA HERRERA: An Image Consultant & Health Coach, Michaela has lived in Santa Fe, New Mexico for the past twelve years. You can visit her health coaching web site www.vitalifline.com, .net, &, .biz. She coaches on weight loss and energy issues. Her image consulting consists of creating confidence by working on self-esteem issues, as well as polishing one's image via hair, make up, posture, etc, for life transitions, job changes, promotions and overall youthfulness. She can be reached for her Image Consulting or Health Coaching at (505) 989-8522 or maherrera7@yahoo.com.

SHARON L HORSTEAD: President of Mindful Heart Learning Inc., Sharon is a Transformational Workshop Leader and personal mentor. Her signature workshop is *Love At Last!* ™ - *From Dreams to Reality* and is based on what worked for her in her own quest to find True Love. Visit her web site at www.mytrueloveatlast.com for articles, tools, products and further information about workshops, teleclasses and coaching for frustrated love-seekers who are willing to try an unconventional but successful approach to meeting their soulmate. Sharon can be reached in Calgary, Canada through her web site or by phone at 1-403-827-3978.

SELIDIA JUNIIS-JOHNSON: Second born daughter of Paul & Margaret Irving, Selidia is a widowed mother of two children, a grandmother, and is retired from the travel industry. She is now following her life's passions, pursuing spiritual studies and sharing Quantum Touch (giving positive spiritual energy) to any who request it. She is a published poet and a leader of Heal Your Life, Achieve Your Dreams Workshops. Selidia resides in Valley Cottage, New York. Contact her by e-mail at sjuniisjohnson@hotmail. com.

KATHRYN JURIC: A dynamic leader and consultant in developing people and businesses to their full potential. Through workshops and coaching, she provides individuals and organizations with tools and strategies to achieve greater success and to create a fulfilling life! Her background includes 20+ years of successful leadership experience at a Fortune 50 Company and an Executive MBA with Honors from New York University. Kathryn has been recognized as an innovative leader and has won several awards. To learn more, visit her web site at www.kathrynjuric.com or call 732-291-0221.

FEZA KARAKAS: An entrepreneur and a healer, Feza recently moved to Turkey after living abroad for 26 years. She is currently in the process of setting up her own workshops in Turkey and writing her own first book. She can be reached at following address: Yali Mahellesi, Diana Sitesi No. 7, Side, Antalya, Turkey. Tel: +90 533 683 7618 e-mail: feza1999@hotmail.com

LIZ KELAHER: Liz works in finance and lives with her teenage son in Sydney, Australia. If you would like to contact Liz her e-mail address is ekelaher@bigpond.net.au.

LYNN KOLL: Owner of Soaring Hearts and Pine Stone Lodge, LLC., Lynn is a Personal Evolution Coach, Energy Practitioner, and Spa Consultant. Soaring Hearts provides individual and group sessions, retreats, playshops, empowerment tools and products to embrace change and make your heart glow with peak energy, joy, and confidence. For more articles and inspiration to live the life of your dreams, visit her web site at www.soaringhearts.net. Lynn can be reached via e-mail at: lynn@soaringhearts.net. Is your heart ready to soar?

DAWN LEVY-MAEDA: President of YOU-TOPIA Healing Arts & Workshops Inc., Dawn is an RNhP (Registered Natural health Practitioner) in a Toronto based clinic where she practices Hot Stone Massage, Thai Yoga Massage, Deep Tissue massage and Reflexology. Due to many experiences involving intuition, trusting in the universe, and affirmations, Dawn is now being trained to lead Heal Your Life, Achieve Your Dreams Workshops, so that she can share these amazing "miracles" with you. For further information you can reach Dawn at www.you-topia.ca

DR. RITA R. MARTINEZ: As owner of Corazon Presentations, Dr. Martinez is a personal coach and spiritual leader in her Phoenix, Arizona community. For further information about her workshops visit her web site at www.corazonpresentations.com. Her work with adults and children in schools may be helpful to your own spiritual or personal growth. Learn to listen to your heart, mind, and soul to reach your highest potential. E-mail her at corazon@cox.net to set up a personal consultation and spiritual healing.

ANNIE MILLER: Life coach, trainer, businesswoman and pre-senter. Annie has a creative background as a chef and still carries passion for great food and wine. Annie is the mother of two children and is journeying as a carer for her terminally ill best friend. Her inspiration is most derived from seeing people of all ages reaching their potential and more, after encouragement to use their own values. Annie lives in Sydney, Australia and can be contacted by e-mail at lightstream@optusnet.com.au or by mail at Lightstream Pty Ltd, PO Box 2107, Boronia Park NSW 2111, Australia.

RENEE MONTEMAYOR: Renee is an actress and healer who balances two of her passions in life joyfully! Best known for playing Briony on BBC's "Grange Hill" she was chosen to represent the show when it won a BAFTA award. Renee's other credits include film, television, and theatre. Between acting commitments, Renee runs a busy private practice and also does workshops and consul-tations at "Mysteries". She's trained in many healing modalities: Reiki, aura-soma, healing breathwork, clairvoyance, tarot/angel card readings, and Heal Your Life, Achieve Your Dreams work-shops. For information on Renee's healing work and workshops go to www.angelic-creations.net. For information on her acting career visit www.reneemontemayor.com.

REV. LA TONIA MUHAMMAD: Rev. Muhammad is the founder of Rebirth International and is available for coaching, group fa-cilitation and speaking engagements. Be coached, be lifted and emerge transformed! She currently resides in Washington, DC and is the *Assistant Minister* at The Inner Visions Full Life Fellowship, *Faculty* at The Inner Visions Institute for Spiritual Development and *Associate Minister* at Union Temple Baptist Church. Contact her directly at 301-873-7124 or www.rebirthinternational.com.

MELISSA ANN PRIVETT: Owner of "Pathworks" located in Detroit, Michigan, Melissa is a Certified Heal Your Life, Achieve Your Dreams Workshop Leader, Keynote Speaker, Spiritual Coach, and Visionary. Her life mission: "to make a difference." Join her newsletter at www.lifepathworkshops.com. It's filled with inspiring articles and transitional tools for creating the life you want! Melissa is available to travel to your city to offer workshops on the following: Heal Your Life, Meditation, Creative Visualization, Anger and Stress Management and a variety of other motivating workshops for inner growth and wellness. Call her for personal healing alternatives (248) 231 8018.

SUSAN DAWN QUEEN: Susan was born and raised in Southern California, where she taught part-time at Golden West College. She received formal psychic training in Northern California at the Berkley Psychic Institute. Susan is a Universal Life minister, and trained in Clinical Hypnotherapy. She is a Reiki Practitioner from the Usui Shiki Ryoho, Reiki Path of Empowerment tradition. Susan is always inspired by her family and their love. She happily resides in California and Georgia, where she continues her healing work with others through teaching workshops, readings, soul coaching, and spiritual guidance. Contact her at 678-714-4677 or visit her web site: www.susanqueen.com.

MICHELE HATFIELD QUESENBERRY: Michele is the creator of the *Gralphabet*™, a fun process used to empower and condition the mind to be grateful. She is a Certified Holistic Spiritual Counselor, Energy Practitioner and Heal Your Life Workshop Leader with ten years of experience facilitating individual and group empowerment programs. Her vocation is dedicated to the integration of emotional, physical, mental and spiritual well-being. Her passion is teaching individuals how to release limiting patterns and replace them with positive empowering ones which attract the life they truly desire. Michele is the founder of Grateful Bits, LLC and Vibrantly Alive! Visit her web site at www.GratefulBits.com.

DELIA REGAN: As a certified teacher of Heal Your Life, Achieve Your Dreams workshops, Delia runs courses and facilitates talks, workshops and seminars. She is also a qualified Life Coach, Reiki Master and practitioner in Aromatherapy Massage, Indian Head Massage, Hopi Ear Candling (Thermo-Auricular massage) and

Emotional Freedom Technique. Delia is inspired and committed in her profession to promote self-healing within the individual and offers the therapies to the work establishment and home with 'Pamper Days'. Living in Liverpool, U.K. she offers her inspirational workshops and talks farther afield. She can be contacted on 44 (0)151 733 9368, E-mail: Anthony@Regan2146.freeserve.co.uk

GEORGINA RODRIGUEZ PAZ: Georgina is a certified Heal Your Life, Achieve Your Dreams workshop leader in Mexico. She has a Personal Development Diploma from Iberoamericana University, and is currently completing her Master's there. Some of the many self-development courses she has participated in are: Silva Mind Control, Dale Carnegie Trainings and Franklin Covey Courses. She has an MBA from Nuevo Leon University in Mexico. She is located in Monterrey, NL Mexico. Phone: (52) 81-10-63-46-49 e-mail: norma_georgina@yahoo.com.mx.

SUSAN ROBERTS: Susan and her husband Stuart Cobb Alexander, run a company dedicated to helping people realise their true potential, utilising a synergistic approach to achieving fulfilment and success. Stuart, a naturopathic nutritionist and fitness consultant, helps clients to attain optimum health and vitality. Susan, a personal development coach and trainer supports clients to achieve what is most important to them. Susan runs workshops and one-to-one coaching programmes, which include Building Confidence, Work/Life Balance, Career Direction and Achieving Ambitions. For tips, tools and more details on nutrition, fitness and personal development programmes visit their web site www. cobbalexander.com or e-mail them at info@cobbalexander.com

BEVERLY STALEY: As a Certified Life Coach, Beverly believes in working with the "whole" person. She uses her extensive education, training and experience in psychology, expressive arts and relationship counseling to enrich her holistic coaching approach. Beverly has developed and presented many self improvement workshops, including Visioning®, Self Esteem and Life Coaching where she helps participants clarify their vision, uncover their passion, then create goals for success. Beverly has a private coaching practice in Orange County, CA but does much of her coaching by phone and is able, therefore, to coach anywhere. She may be contacted at 949-459-1080 or e-mail: bevstaley@cox.net.

ANITA STAPLETON-MIROLO: Anita is a qualified Life Coach, Heal Your Life Workshop Leader, Meditation Teacher and Reiki Practitioner and holds a degree in psychology and philosophy. Located in Dublin, Ireland, Anita offers regular personal development classes, workshops, group coaching and personal coaching in and around the Dublin area and is available to travel to other parts of Ireland. In the long term, Anita plans to record guided meditation CDs and publish self-help articles and books. For more information, please visit her web site at www.asm-healing.com. To contact Anita, please telephone (+353) 01 8339951 or e-mail anita@asm-healing.com

STEPHANIE SWINK: Owner of *Loving Life Services* and co-owner of *Organizing Angels* in Orange County, CA, Stephanie is a spiritual counselor, Authentic Happiness coach and Professional Organizer (www.yourorganizingangels.com). She has been in the business of assisting people in positively transforming their lives for many years. As personal assistant to author Louise Hay, she responded to thousands of "Dear Louise" letters and simultaneously graduated as a Licensed Religious Science Practitioner from Holmes Institute in 1999. Through her seminars, retreats and organizing services, Stephanie fulfills her hearts desire of supporting people in truly loving their lives! Contact her at (949) 230-9102 or visit www.stephanieswink.com.

CARRIE THOMAS: Carrie offers intuitive healing (including phone sessions), and self-development workshops. She is fully qualified in 'The Work' (Byron Katie's wonderful method for quieting stressful thoughts), facilitating individual sessions (including phone) and workshops. Visit www.touchwoodspirit.com or ring +44(0)1792-522443 for more information, including her intuitive healing that incorporates channelled divine wisdom, and the use of Touchwood Flower Essences to help ease you through stressful periods in your life. Workshops include: healing, intuition, change, 'The Work', forgiveness, self-esteem, angels and spiritual development. Located in Touchwood, Swansea, South Wales, Carrie also travels to other venues to offer her workshops and healing.

YVONNE VERNON: Yvonne is a teacher of divine and spiritual integration through God and His angels in our lives. Sharing her gifted insights she inspires and teaches us to align our consciousness with divine consciousness realizing peace, love, balance and harmony bringing whole healing to the body, mind and spirit. She is presently authoring a book, *Divine Intervention for Healing*. Visit her web site at www.angels-are-real.com for information on her courses, powerful faith building tele-sessions, summer solstice retreats, private angelic messages and products. Or call her at (604) 465-7517. She is located in Vancouver, British Columbia, Canada.

CORENE WALKER: Corene lives in Cambridge, New Zealand with her two wonderful children. Professionally, Corene is a Corporate Coach, Graduate of CoachU University, USA, and a Heal Your Life, Achieve Your Dreams workshop leader. Her leadership experience includes a background in human resources, health and wellness and a solid understanding of the fundamentals of human behaviour and interpersonal dynamics. She coaches virtually allowing her to work with corporate teams and individuals worldwide. Corene's strength is in working with people to create a culture of caring truth, high performance, advanced communication, inspirational team leadership and high emotional intelligence. E-mail: corene@empoweringgroup.net. T: +64-7-8232901, www. empoweringgroup.net.

SARAH WATERS: Sarah is a business woman, teacher and spiritual channel working throughout the UK, whose aim is to help people reach their highest potential. She is dedicated to her own spiritual growth and knows that by doing her own inner work she can help heal the world. Sarah can be contacted by e-mail: sarah@healingfeelings.co.uk.

MARDI ZEUNERT: As the principal of her business, Inside Life, Mardi is a personal coach and facilitator. She also works in her other business as an author, project manager and marketer. Mardi is passionate about people development and is a qualified Heal Your Life, Achieve Your Dreams workshop leader. Her passion is personal coaching, working one-on-one with people to assist them to realise their dreams and become who they want to be in their life. Contact Mardi for further information on her life leadership packages: Inside Life, PO Box 193, Goodwood 5034, South Australia. Mobile: + 61 (0) 0438 886 522 e-mail: pezed@senet.com.au

Bibliography:

Books cited in the stories

Foundation for Inner Peace.
A Course in Miracles. 1992

Capacchione, Ph.D., Lucia:
The Power of Your Other Hand. New Page Books,
2001
The Creative Journal. New Page Books, 2001
Recovery of Your Inner Child. Fireside, 1991

Emoto, Dr. Masara:
Messages from Water. Hado Publishing, 2003

Epstein, Donald:
12 Stages of Healing. Amber-Allen Publishing,
1994

Hay, Louise:
You Can Heal Your Life. Hay House, 1984

Harold Kushner:
When Bad Things Happen to Good People. Anchor,
2004

Moore, Thomas:
Care of the Soul. Harper paperbacks. 1994

Siegel, M.D., Bernie:
Love, Medicine and Miracles. Harper Paperbacks,
1990

Stone, Hal and Sidra:
Embracing Your Inner Critic. Harper San Francisco,
1993

Tagore, Rabindranath:
Stray Birds. Kessinger Publishing, 2004

Weekes, Dr. Claire:
Hope and Help for Your Nerves. Signet Books, 1991

Weiss, Brian:
Many Lives, Many Masters. Fireside, 1988

Williamson, Marianne:
A Return to Love. Harper Paperbacks, 1996

About Patricia Crane, Ph.D. :

Patricia is an author, speaker, and workshop leader. Her first book, *Ordering From the Cosmic Kitchen: The Essential Guide to Powerful, Nourishing Affirmations,* has received enthusiastic reviews. She discovered the life-affirming principles shared in that book through her own personal search for meaning and purpose. A meditation practice for many years has been the foundation for her growth.

With a strong desire to help others, she initially pursued an educational route, earning a Ph.D. in social psychology with a specialty focus on wellness programs at the worksite (primarily stress management). For several years she taught stress management courses at the university level and gave corporate workshops. But her heart was yearning to share something deeper. Having attended numerous workshops with some of the premier spiritual leaders of our time and studied personal development and spiritual books, she began to offer workshops in meditation, the mind/body connection, prosperity, Reiki Natural Healing, creative visualization, effective affirmations, breathwork, and more. Her work with Louise Hay resulted in leading international workshops and creating a powerful training program for personal growth workshop leaders.

In 1995 she met life partner Rick Nichols, and they began traveling and teaching together, plus collaborating on personal growth products. They now live in a beautiful country setting in north San Diego County on a seven acre ranch, complete with an avocado grove. The serene view across the valley nurtures and rejuvenates them on a daily basis.

Patricia's intention is to continue sharing a message of personal empowerment in co-creation with Spirit. She is committed to the expansion of the heart for personal and planetary healing.

ABOUT RICK NICHOLS:

Rick Nichols, a principal partner of Heart Inspired Presentations and an expert on human potential, is an author, storyteller and international speaker. With his inspirational, warm, and humorous style Rick has captivated audiences around the world. He is a speaker of many facets, at once a storyteller, poet, and philosopher, as well as a teacher and student of life.

Raised by a pair of alcoholic combatants in a domestic war zone along with five siblings, Rick learned much about coping with adversity early in life. Upon awakening the morning of his 17th birthday he had to face the fact that while others of his age were about to graduate high school, he was failing the 9th grade. It was on that day that Rick leaped from one war zone to another, as he joined the US Navy and went to Vietnam; there his education really began. He learned important things that the public school systems didn't teach: self-esteem, teamwork, cooperation, and compassion. One of the most important things he learned was that he is capable of learning, and that he has value; nobody had ever told him that before.

On a life mission to "Inspire people the world over to a higher level of thinking about who they are, what they've got, and how to bring themselves more fully into the world," Rick presents programs designed to shift a person's perspective, which opens them to a deeper self-awareness and greater potential for a fulfilling life. The rich diversity of Rick's salt and pepper background is sprinkled throughout his presentations. He has experienced the highs and lows of life, learned how to make the best of it all, and is willing to intimately share it with his audiences.

WORKSHOPS, KEYNOTES, AND SEMINARS:

Patricia and Rick offer a variety of powerful programs and products for personal growth. For a current
schedule and to see all their products, please visit their
main web site, www.heartinspired.com. They are available to travel to your group for presentations. Their
workshops, keynotes, and seminars include:

Creating Wealth From the Inside Out

**Wisdom of the Ages from the Land of Oz
and Beyond**

**Heal Your Life, Achieve Your Dreams
Workshop Leader Training**

Stress Management

Healing Breathwork

Success Strategies for Women on the Go

The Magic of Believing in Yourself

Contact them at (800) 969-4584 or (760) 728-8783 or
write to P.O. Box 1081, Bonsall, CA 92003.
E-mail patricia@heartinspired.com
or rick@heartinspiredcom.

VISIT US ON THE INTERNET:

The following web sites will give you complete information on all of the programs we are currently offering. Be sure to take advantage of the many free online training opportunities you will find. You may also want to subscribe to our free weekly inspirational Internet magazine, Monday Morning HeartBeats. It is the perfect way to get your week started on a positive note. Free QuickTips for more successful living are provided every Friday to get you ready for the weekend. We are sure you will enjoy the free inspirational flash movie presentations.

www.HeartInspired.com
Our flag ship web site and the hub for all the sites listed below. From here you can learn all about us and what we offer that will be of value to you.

www.ChangeInsideOut.com
Take our online courses in meditation, creating wealth, affirmations, conscious weight loss, and more... all for one easy, affordable lifetime membership fee.

www.TakingABreather.com
Relax and enjoy the peace and beauty of nature, music and art. This four minute experience will instantly put peace and tranquility into your life, no matter how hectic it has been. Learn simple techniques for managing stress.

www.MessagesFromTheAngels.com
Angels are the part of God that appear to us on earth in a way we can understand. The angels constantly

tell of joy, peace and love, for that is the only story they have to tell.

Take a moment for communion with the angels. They will inspire you with a renewed faith that all is well.

www.OrderingFromtheCosmicKitchen.com

Learn how to create and use powerful affirmations to improve your life in every way. Be sure and sign up here for Patricia's powerful e-course on affirmations and preview a chapter of her book, *Ordering from the Cosmic Kitchen: The Essential Guide to Powerful, Nourishing Affirmations.*

www.HYLTeachers.com

A directory of trained Heal Your Life, Achieve Your Dreams teachers worldwide. Learn how you too can be certified to lead Heal Your Life, Achieve Your Dreams workshops.

www.ScienceOfGettingRichNow.com

Learn the mental and spiritual principles for becoming rich. We are always in choice, the Universe provides an abundance of opportunities and then leaves it entirely up to each individual whether to accept or reject them.

www.SuccessForBiz.com

Success Strategies for Life and Business.

Business topics include empowerment, self-esteem, creativity, stress management, workplace wellness, communication skills and presentation skills.

Personal growth topics include releasing old beliefs, increasing prosperity, finding your ideal life work, and more.

Other Books from Heart Inspired Presentations:

Ordering from the Cosmic Kitchen:
The Essential Guide to Powerful Nourishing Affirmations
by Patricia Crane, Ph.D.

All 5 star reviews on Amazon.com!

Learn how to create and use powerful affirmations to improve your life in every way.

One hundred sixty pages in twelve chapters filled with success stories from cosmic orders and instructions on how to order up the things you want, need and deserve from life. Order your copy today!

"If you're ready to lovingly nurture yourself with positive affirmations, here's the book for you."

-Mark Victor Hansen
Co-creator, #1 New York Times best-selling series
Chicken Soup for the Soul

In the Flow of Life:
How to Create and Build Beautiful Indoor Water Fountains
by Rick Nichols

Learn how to create and build your own beautiful and soothing water fountains for as little as $25.00 in materials!

"This is a most practical guide to making your own wondrous creation: your own personalized water feature. Enjoy!"

-Terah Kathryn Collins
Author of The Western Guide to Feng Shui